THE
WOODLAND
GARDEN

THE WOODLAND GARDEN

A Practical Guide

Raymond Foster

With Line Illustrations by Rosemary Wise

WARD LOCK LIMITED · LONDON

© Text R. Foster 1980

© Illustrations Ward Lock Ltd. 1980

First published in Great Britain in 1980
by Ward Lock Limited, 116 Baker Street,
London W1M 2BB, a Pentos Company.

House editors Denis Ingram and Deborah Maby
Layout by Bridget Tisdall

Text filmset in Bembo

Printed and bound in Great Britain by
Fakenham Press Limited,
Fakenham, Norfolk

British Library Cataloguing in Publication Data

Foster, Raymond
    The woodland garden.
    1. Ornamental trees
    2. Landscape gardening
    I. Title
    712'.6   SB435

ISBN 0–7063–5990–9

Contents

Preface

The people of the Western World love trees, but have tended to take them for granted—until now, for in recent years a string of disasters seems to have struck our trees: elms have almost disappeared from the scene in many parts of the world; oaks and beeches are threatened, and diseases of other trees are widespread; a season of unprecedented drought has caused many losses; and long winters followed by atrocious spring weather conditions have all had their effect.

By tradition, woodland gardens have been large—almost on a forest scale—and rather remote from the average plot. The tendency has been to regard trees in the garden as 'one-off' items, almost as if they were statues or sundials. But this book sets out to show how the best woodland principles can be applied successfully on a small scale.

Landscape planners and those concerned professionally with conserving or creating anew the woodland environment may find something of value in this book, but it is intended primarily for those many new house owners who, faced with a stark, muddy rectangle of land, feel they would like to create something special.

It is not such a long-term project as might be supposed. A woodland garden designed and planted on the principles outlined in this book will look good the very first season. In five years time it will be beautiful, and in ten years the ageless succession of woodland maturity will have become established. The environment, both for us and for the countless tiny creatures which share our planet, will have been, in some small measure, enriched.

R.F.

Acknowledgement

All line drawings are by Rosemary Wise.
Figures 33, 41, 42 and 43 are redrawn
from diagrams supplied by the author.

Glossary

Bole: The trunk of a tree.

Bract: A kind of leaf which often has the appearance of a flower.

Broadleaf: A non-coniferous tree, usually with typical, flat leaves.

Bulbil: A small immature bulb, often formed at the base of mature bulbs, or on stems above ground.

Calcareous: Limy.

Calcifuge, calcifugous: Lime-hating.

Cambium: The actively growing part of a tree between the wood and the bark.

Canopy: The leafy cover formed by the linking up of branches.

Climax, climactic: The stable type of vegetation attained through forest succession.

Compound leaf: A leaf that is divided into several leaflets.

Conifer: A cone-bearing tree, usually with narrow, needle-like leaves.

Coppice: Trees or shrubs that have been cut back to produce several small shoots.

Crown: Of a tree, the branches and foliage; of a herbaceous plant, the solid part above ground.

Deciduous: Having leaves which are shed during winter.

Dominant: Tending to outgrow and suppress neighbouring trees.

Evergreen: Having leaves which are persistent throughout the year.

Family: A group of related genera.

Genus, genera: A group or groups of closely related species.

Glaucous: Coated with greyish bloom, like a grape.

Hardwood: A broadleaf tree.

Heel: A small piece of older wood retained at the base of a side-shoot that has been pulled off to make a cutting.

High forest: Composed of trees allowed to grow to maturity.

Humus: Organic material in the soil.

Indigenous: Truly native.

Internodal cutting: A cutting without a node or bud at its base.

Leader, leading shoot: The main upright shoot of a tree, or occasionally of a branch.

Leaflet: One of the small leaves that make up a compound leaf.

Loam: A balanced type of soil which includes both coarse sand and clay.

Naturalized: An introduced plant that is able to reproduce itself without assistance.

Node, nodal cutting: A joint or leaf bud, used as the base of a cutting.

Over-storey: The highest canopy layers of a forest.

Panicle: A flower spike composed of separate clusters.

Parasite, parasitic: Feeding on live matter.

Pedunculate: The flowers or fruits have stalks.

Persistent: Remaining on the plant.

pH: A measure of soil acidity and alkalinity.

Photosynthesis: The process by which plants manufacture food through sunlight.

Pinnate: Having an evenly compound leaf.

Pioneer, pioneering: The first plants to appear on bare land.

Pleach: To train and intertwine branches to form a hedge.

Pollard: A tree that has been caused to coppice at crown height.

Pure stand: Woodland composed of one kind of tree only.

Raceme: A flower spike with solitary, stalked flowers.

Rhizome: A type of swollen, underground stem.

Saprophyte, saprophytic: Feeding on dead plant matter.

Sessile: Stalkless.

Species: A group of individuals with the same distinguishing features.

Stamens: The male, pollen-producing parts of a flower.

Standard: A young tree with a clear stem of at least 1·5 m (5 ft).

Stolon: A type of shoot that spreads at or below ground level.

Storey: One of several canopy layers in a forest.

Striated: Striped.

Strike, struck: To put out new roots, or persuade a cutting to take root.

Succession: The natural progression from pioneer to climax vegetation.

Sucker: A young plant growing from the root of an old plant.

Summer-green: Bearing leaves during the summer.

Underplanting: Planting beneath a tree canopy.

Under-storey: The lower canopy layers of a forest.

Variety, varietal: A consistent variation within a species.

Whip transplant: A newly planted tree that has not yet formed crown branches.

Winter-green: Bearing leaves during the winter.

1

The Integrity of the Woods

The structure of a woodland is a subtle, living entity. It is the balance between trees, shrubs, herbs and ground-covering plants, a flourishing of nature; a maturity complete and wholesome that we wish, not to emulate, but to recreate when we construct a woodland garden. It is no mere haphazard arrangement, though it might appear so. The forest is regulated in layers: the tallest trees whose branches and leaves, in forming the uppermost canopy, are presented to the sun; and those slightly less tall, and able to bear a certain amount of shade, may conveniently be classed together and termed the over-storey. Small trees and shrubs able to thrive below this tall canopy may be grouped with the shade-bearing herbs at ground level, and together termed the under-storey.

We can appreciate the many factors involved in building up an ornamental woodland community by understanding something about the natural woodland types themselves for, in many parts of the world, climate and soil work spontaneously towards the formation of high forest as a climactic vegetational goal.

In North America for example, a natural forest succession persists on uncultivated land anywhere east of the Great Plains, and wherever there is moisture enough to support tree life in the west, too. In Britain, the rainfall is more evenly distributed, and the woodland types are more clearly differentiated. Indeed, in ancient times virtually the whole of England, Wales, Ireland and Scotland, below the tree-line at about six hundred metres, was clad in a mantle of trees and shrubs.

Of this British forest, the greatest part was oak wood, which was itself divided into two types, corresponding with the two native British oak trees: the stalked oak, so called because the acorns have stalks, and the durmast or sessile oak, with stalkless acorns. Other natural woodland types are named after their dominant tree species, as the beech and ash woods, or after their soil or site type, as the heath and mountain woods.

Lowland Oak Woods

Stalked oak is the dominant species in the midlands and south of England, on the richer, deeper soil. Associated with this oak are ash, birch, maple, cherry and alder, in varying proportions according to the nature of the countryside. Growing beneath these tall trees as a second storey are holly, yew and a few others such as the wild service and the crab apple. Below these as a shrub layer we have principally hazel, hawthorn, elder, dogwood, privet, guelder rose and, especially in damp situations, the osier, the grey and the goat willows. Ivy and honeysuckle are typical climbers in this type of woodland, and below the shrubs there are often clumps of brambles and ferns.

There is an equivalent to this woodland type in the eastern oak woods of the United States, which formerly flourished with their associated species—the American chestnut and the yellow poplar, known to British gardeners as the tulip tree.

The ground-hugging layers of herbs are particularly rich in species in these lowland forests, and the herbs themselves form natural strata through their adaptation to individual light requirements—and their food requirements, for natural stratification of species occurs underground also, with the roots functioning at different levels in the soil so that all the members of a community can survive and flourish. There is a seasonal adaptation, too, among woodland herbs: because the natural oak wood is deciduous, light intensity is at its greatest during winter and early spring, and at its least during the warmest season. Some herbs such as common bugle, ground ivy, wood sorrel, wood sanicle and yellow dead nettle grow new leaves in the autumn as the light increases on the forest floor, and take advantage of the shade-free winter months by staying green so that the process of photosynthesis can continue.

Only a few woodland herbs are summer-green and deciduous in the same way as most of the trees and shrubs in the upper storeys. Many flourish, sometimes spectacularly, before the oak fully opens its leaves in the spring, and may then wither and remain dormant during the period of full shade. Examples of this pattern of behaviour may include the bluebell, whose sheets of colour really typify the oak wood in spring; celandine; and the primrose also behaves in this manner when growing beneath the canopies of forest trees; violet; wood anemone; and wild garlic, which sometimes carpets the wood in damp situations. Other herbs again are truly evergreen, such as periwinkle, hellebore and iris. Ivy, of course, is evergreen, and so are several carpeting shrubs. In woodland gardening we can take full advantage of all these adaptations, and we are not limited to native species, for we have the forests of the world from which to choose.

Upland Oak Woods

Sessile oak woods are typical of northern and western England and Wales. In varying proportions according to the site these ancient forests also contained ash, rowan, birch, service tree and cherry, with yew and holly as common under-storey trees. Hawthorn, elder, hazel, spindle tree and the small willows formed the upper shrub layer.

Modification by the hand of man has been intense over the centuries, but every deciduous wood and copse still clearly relates to the primitive pattern, especially when planting in the past has been limited to the native tree species. There is an equivalent forest type in the northern United States and in Canada, where the indigenous oaks have an admixture of maple, birch and hemlock.

These upland oak woods shelter many species of ferns, including bracken, which thrives—or rampages—in inverse proportion to the density of the tree canopy. Brambles are common and may be intimidatingly thick in some areas. On the forest floor again are bluebell, primrose, violet, wild strawberry, rosebay willow herb and foxglove—the last two always ready to take advantage of any clearings that may appear. Rosebay is also known as 'fireweed' because it so loves newly burnt-over clearings, and is usually the first plant to colonize them by means of its airborne seeds. Stinging nettles also are often poised to colonize disturbed land—perhaps that which has been cultivated or used for stock-keeping.

Heath Woods

The sandy heaths in southern and south-eastern England often support distinctive types of woodland. The dominant tree species is often birch, sometimes in association with the oaks—often a hybrid form between the durmast and the stalked oaks—and with pine. Birch is one of the hardiest of trees, flourishing on very poor sites which may not support the oaks satisfactorily; on better soil, the birch wood type usually represents a transitional phase in forest development. A mature birch casts very little shade, and itself is unable to grow when shaded out by other trees. It is also a comparatively small tree, and these are all factors which combine to allow other tree species to encroach, to grow up through the light shade, to spread their canopies over the birch crowns and thus, eventually, to take over the forest. In this sense, the birch occupies approximately the same status among trees as the rosebay willow herb does among smaller plants: its rapid growth, the wind-borne seeds freely produced and germinating readily, ensure that the birch is the first tree species to recover following a severe fire or drastic forest clearance. Where birches do form the dominant tree species, shrubby undergrowth and the ground-layers of herbs are luxurious on account of the very light shade. However, because the soil is usually poor, sandy and very acid, these are heath plants: gorse, bracken, heather and fine grasses.

Scots pine is also a pioneering tree species in these conditions, for when the cones open the winged seeds may travel quite some distance and they, also, germinate readily. Light demanders like the birch, young pines will also take over birch forest if conditions are right, and they have done so on several of the sandy commons around south London.

European sycamore occupies a position midway between the pioneering and the climactic tree types, and in many places it may seed itself so prolifically as to comprise the dominant species. However, sycamore does not feature in the overall picture of British primitive forest, because the species has only recently been introduced—it was a rare tree even at the time of Cromwell's Civil Wars. Sweet chestnut too sometimes forms almost pure woods on the sandy heath soil, and this again is not truly native, though it has been in Britain since Roman times.

Mountain Woods

The ancient Caledonian pine forests were the forerunners of today's grouse moor and mountain grazing land. Scattered remnants of this natural coniferous forest still exist here and there both in Scotland and Wales. Where pines are growing densely, as we can see in the modern plantations, a thick ground layer of undecomposed needles is formed, and plants are very few or absent. Mountain forests in North America include areas of pure spruce and fir—trees which also form a very dense canopy and deep leaf litter so that few plants can invade them once they are well established. As soon as openings occur, shrubby plants make their appearance; bilberry and the heathers which cover large expanses of British uplands, and mountain cranberry which occurs both in North America and in Scotland, as a forest ground cover which enjoys moderate shade from well-spaced trees. Bilberry demands more light than mountain cranberry, but not as much as heather, and when fire or forest clearing takes place, other factors being equal, the heather usually spreads at these plants' expense.

Pure birch wood also occurs in Scotland and in north England; in the Highlands it sometimes forms the altitudinal forest limit, with fine mountain grasses covering the ground beneath.

Beech Woods

The beech tree seeds itself readily only on certain types of chalk and limestone in the southern part of England, although as a planted tree it will grow well on most soil types. Where the site is really suited to it, it will dominate every other tree species and eventually form almost pure beech woods, as it has on areas of the Cotswolds, the Chilterns and the Downs. Deep chalk soils where the beech can get its roots in firmly are the favoured situations. Ash, cherry, yew and holly also like this type of site, but so dense is the canopy and so heavy the shade cast by the beech that they must survive on sufferance only. Yew and holly sometimes form an under-storey, but in typical cases so little light is able to reach the ground beneath a close stand of beech, that it may be completely bare of the shrub and herb layers common to most other woodland types. Wherever clearings or gaps do occur, herbs such as yellow dead nettle, woodruff, violet, wild strawberry and the grasses are quick to colonize.

Young beech trees themselves endure heavy shade, and for this reason are frequently underplanted in woods other than beech woods, where they can eventually form a pure stand.

Ash Woods

The same type of limestone soils are favoured by the ash, whose natural range in Britain extends well beyond that of the beech. Where the ranges of the two species overlap and there is an element of competition, their very different natures ensure that the beech will predominate, for the ash casts only a very light shade. In the ash's favour are its ability to grow rapidly to a great height, while its winged seeds ensure a far quicker natural spread of the species than the heavy beech mast will allow.

The very light shade cast by the ash ensures a well-stocked undergrowth of shrubs and herbs, and the taller native trees which thrive in its company include the aspen, wych elm, field maple and yew. Shrubs include the small willows, dogwood, privet, briars and brambles, and ivy is abundant as a climber and ground coverer. Honeysuckle may be plentiful, and in some areas this type of woodland supports wild clematis which may festoon the trees on the edge of every large clearing.

The white starry flowers of wild garlic often blend with bluebell and red campion to carpet these woods in May and June. Other herbs at ground level include dog's mercury, woodruff, celandine, and ground ivy when the under-storey and shrub layers are not too dense, for the overhead canopy is so light that yews may be frequent, and the grey and goat willows and privet may form thickets dark enough to exclude many summergreen herbs.

Ash may combine with either of the two oaks to form mixed woodland, but although it will grow on those acid soils where the oak thrives, ash is not really at home on them. In the wetter parts of its range, ash wood may run into almost pure alder woodland, a specialized type which once covered considerable areas of the fens and river valleys.

Ornamental Woods

Certainly, woodlands which are left to their own devices today, provided they are composed of native species, soon become indistinguishable from the primeval pattern. But much of the wooded British countryside owes its beauty to the wealth of foreign trees that have been introduced and planted since the time of the Roman occupation. Much, also, of that 'typically English' landscape of plantations and broad-crowned parkland trees came into being only during the eighteenth century, when the fashion for land-scaped grounds reached an all-time peak in the hands of Capability Brown and Humphrey Repton.

Parkland landscaping was not the beginning of woodland gardening, although several of those early Georgian plantations may have become the majestic framework of our system a hundred years later. It was largely as a matter of necessity that the concept of woodland gardening arose in the great gardens of Britain around the beginning of the twentieth century. It was a period of determined botanical exploration, and many exciting new plants were being introduced—rhododendron, eucryphia, camellia, pieris—most of them from the forests of the world. British gardens tended, then as now, to be over-limed. But it is in the nature of forest to luxuriate the more, and to support a greater variety of plants, when the soil that supports it is rather on the acid side of neutral. Indeed, the constant addition of leaf mould tends to acidify alkaline soils—or at least to form a shallow layer of acid mould overlying the alkaline subsoil; the surface rooting systems of calcifugous under-storey plants such as the rhododendrons are well adapted to meet this situation. Consequently, these promising new shrubs planted to show their paces and prominently sited in the sunniest borders merely languished and turned yellow. The first head gardener to banish the homesick newcomers despairingly to the woodland fringe was so impressed by their speedy recovery, their instant response in the shape of healthy new growth and spectacular flower, that the news quickly spread from garden to garden. A whole new understanding of plant environmental requirements was initiated.

The great woodland gardens that ensued: Bodnant, the Saville Gardens at Windsor Great Park, Benenden Grange, Lochinch, Penjerrick, are all full of examples that those who garden on a more modest scale might study and possibly reproduce.

Very few houses are able to boast of a patch of woodland as a garden; but there is no good reason why this type of gardening should be limited to already existing woodland. A tiny neglected orchard—perhaps only two or three trees—is a good base around which to plan something special. But even this is not essential. The great majority of gardens attached to new houses comprise bare, treeless rectangles; and it is just these unpromising, depressing sites that can be and have been transformed into flourishing woodland groves.

A useful preliminary step is to take a simple pH test of the soil, if not to decide what plants are to be grown, at least to eliminate those which are out of the question. In the case of trees, whose roots are going to penetrate perhaps quite deeply into the soil, it is as well to know what is going to grow, and what is not. With smaller plants, there are ways round the problem. Lavish use can be made of peat and leaf mould—from trees that have been grown on acid soil, otherwise their leaves will be alkaline, too—and chemicals can be used, with care. A neutral pH reaction is 7; anything greater than this is alkaline, while any number smaller shows an acid reaction. In practice, it will very rarely be necessary to raise the pH value when gardening for a woodland effect. Nine times out of ten the problem will be too high a reading, and therefore too alkaline a soil.

To raise the pH is commonplace; many people add lime to their gardens almost by tradition. But lime is anathema to calcifugous plants such as the rhododendrons. If it should be necessary to raise the pH—or reduce the acidity—of sites that we intend to use for growing shrubs such as these, the safest way of doing it is to add gypsum to the soil at the rate of about 25 g/sq m (0·74 oz/sq yd), to raise the pH reading by one point.

When it is required to lower the pH or further acidify the soil, an acceptable way of achieving this is by adding 60 g/sq m (2 oz/sq yd) of aluminium sulphate, well worked into the topsoil, and this should lower the pH reading by one point. In circumstances where this is found to be necessary, the site is almost certain to need the addition of peat as well, and this should be added liberally. Peat is expensive, of course, but a great saving can be made if the planting work proceeds piecemeal, by groups, or even by individual plants, a bed at a time.

Assuming a new garden plot with no tree cover, the first basic essential is to plant reasonably quick-growing standard trees to form the crown framework. Smallish trees such as rowan, birch, cherries and some of the maples, are ideal. We can always plan to introduce yet taller trees to grow through this low canopy, eventually to create a top storey, but the first priority is to bring about a woodland environment on a small scale. Occasionally, trees with a very rapid rate of growth and which are otherwise quite unsuitable for garden use, may be planted to supply temporary shade, the intention being to remove them later on. The poplars are usually chosen for this role. But when this is done, it is essential to ensure that the subsequent part of the plan is put into effect: they really must be removed the moment their purpose has been fulfilled, otherwise their presence will become a menace. Poplars that have been allowed to become dominant in the garden will not only spoil the woodland environmental balance they were intended to foster—they will threaten adjacent houses as well, for in dry weather their thirsty roots draw moisture out of the clay below the foundations, causing it to shrink.

Once a light tracery of shade has been established—and a sparse canopy it is indeed bound to be for the first few years—the main under-storey shrubs may be introduced. Trees planted in the form of standards do not necessarily outgrow others of seedling or whip size planted at the same time; sometimes the reverse is true because, by and large, the older a transplant is, the more its growth is liable to be checked by the move. But in this case at least, choosing standard trees gives us the great advantage of having already created a certain amount of shade; supplementary planting can then begin immediately.

The most convenient way to carry out this supplementary planting is to dig small beds here and there as required—they need be only a metre or so square for most shrubs—and the soil within these individual beds may be worked and treated to suit the intended occupant; there is no need to treat the whole area uniformly.

While this basic work is in progress, the rest of the garden may still be full of vegetables or annuals, or sown to grass—on a long-term catch-crop basis. In this way, the woodland environment will evolve gradually and painlessly, with new plants being introduced as conditions become right for them; the only stipulation being that once a bed containing shrubs or a new tree has been established, every effort should be made to keep the immediate surrounds free from grass and perennial weeds, if necessary by using a weedkiller containing paraquat, such as Weedol. Even the most vigorous invaders such as ground elder will succumb if their top growth is killed often enough, especially if they put in an appearance during the winter months and can be tackled then, when their resistance and powers of recovery are at their lowest ebb.

The list of trees in the section which follows includes types ranging from the best small trees for introduction into a bare garden plot, to the forest giants which we may be lucky enough to have to plant under. The owner of a piece of woodland starts with a wonderful advantage—though a certain element of choice has already been taken away. The brief descriptions of forest types will have suggested where the advantages and disadvantages lie. In existing woodland, it will probably be found necessary to remove certain of the trees before underplanting can take place, and great care should be taken in the selection of these. As a rule, it is best to concentrate one's attention on the pattern of branches and leaves high in the woodland canopy. In forestry, this is the principle of 'crown thinning'—in making his choice, the forester is looking, not at the stems and their spacing, but up into the crowns, at their intertwining and their relationships one with another. His endeavour is to 'see' how the canopy would look after any particular tree has been removed. In this way, he can gauge precisely how much extra light will be allowed to reach the woodland floor.

Our aim will be similar, but more complex. We have to bear in mind not only the optimum development of those trees to remain after thinning, but also the way we want our garden to develop, stage by stage. The forester, more often than not, is working within the highly restrictive environment of pure-stand or balanced-mixture plantation. We, on the other hand, are hoping to recreate the complicated structure of natural woodland, and we have most of the plants of the temperate world at our disposal.

2
The Over-Storey

This chapter describes some of the trees which may be used to form the framework of a woodland garden. The list is by no means complete. As a selection it must be based, partly at least, on personal preference, but only those trees which should prove hardy and easy to grow on a wide range of sites have been included.

Propagation

Many of the trees and shrubs are normally propagated by layering, but this is easier in nurseries where stock plants can be kept cut back to provide a plentiful supply of suitable shoots. In the case of an established tree, it is often impossible to bring a branch into contact with the ground. In the past, owners of valuable stock trees such as the rarer magnolias, have even built scaffolding around the outer branches so that the shoots can be layered directly into pots. Fortunately, there is a much more convenient method known as 'air layering', and under normal conditions this method may be tried on any species which will not take readily from cuttings.

The operation is usually carried out in the spring. A cut is made upwards, starting immediately below a bud or node, and the resultant tongue is wedged open with a twist of sphagnum moss that has been dipped in hormone rooting powder. Then a 15 cm (6 in) length of stem—half above the cut and half below it—is swathed in more sphagnum moss to make a cylinder or ball which is bandaged securely with polythene film and sealed with sticky tape. The moss must be moist, and the final seal should be airtight so that this moisture will not be lost. Peat or some similar material can be used instead of moss. When roots have grown they can be seen through the polythene, and the stem can then be cut below the root-ball, the polythene removed, and the new plant potted up.

Abies

The silver firs, giant evergreen conifers which make impressive specimen trees. Propagation is always by seed, and the large, cylindrical cones disintegrate when the seed is ripe. There are many species and varieties, and the best of these for garden use are:

A. grandis: A very fast-growing, 75 m (250 ft) tree whose dark green leaves are produced in distinctive, horizontal tiers. It thrives in areas that experience a high annual rainfall, is a good shade bearer, does not like industrial pollution, but tolerates a limy soil.

A. nordmanniana: A 60 m (200 ft) tree with tiered, downward-sweeping branches and stout needles that lend a bristly appearance to the twigs. It is tolerant of most soil types.

A. procera: A magnificent 60 m (200 ft) tree with glaucous-grey, crowded, bristly needles and immense cylindrical cones. It grows very well in deep soils with a good rainfall, but will not tolerate lime.

Acer

The maples: a large group of very ornamental trees ranging in size from dwarf trees or shrubs, such as the many forms of *A. palmatum*, to giant forest trees such as the European sycamore. The maples are easily grown in any reasonably good soil, acid or limy. They are all deciduous. The chief identifying feature of the genus is the distinctive fruit which consists of a pair of winged seeds. Propagation is normally by seed, but this often proves to be infertile, in which case shoots must be grafted onto seedling stocks of other similarly-sized species.

A. campestre: The British field maple, a small tree about 7–8 m (23–27 ft) high—or occasionally taller when it takes its place as a canopy tree. The crown has a neat, rounded shape, and the five-lobed leaves are about 7·5 cm (3 in) wide. Varieties of use in the garden are 'Postelense' with yellow leaves; 'Pulverentulum' with white-spotted leaves; 'Schwerinii' with leaves that are purple in the spring, and 'Variegatum' with white-margined leaves.

A. capillipes: A tree of some 9 m (30 ft) with handsome, striped bark and good autumn foliage colour. The three-lobed leaves are 10 cm (4 in) wide and have red stalks and veins. The flowers and seed-bunches are green.

A. circinatum: A wide-spreading maple up to 9 m (30 ft) high. The leaves have seven or nine lobes and are about 10 cm (4 in) wide, colouring well before falling. An attractive tree with smooth, reddish bark, and purple and white flowers in April, followed by the winged keys.

A. crataegifolium: An upright, 6 m (20 ft) tree with striped bark. The three- or five-lobed leaves measure about 7·5 cm (3 in) wide by 4 cm (1½ in) long, and there are good autumn colours. Variety 'Veitchii' has leaves that are variegated with pink and white.

Acer circinatum (maple). The winged seeds (one of the maples' distinguishing features) follow the purple and white flowers, which are borne in April.

A. davidii: A spreading tree up to 10 m (33 ft) high, with orna-mental striped bark, drooping bunches of winged seeds and some autumn colour. The leaves are not lobed, and measure about 15×5 cm (6×2 in).

A. ginnala: A small tree, around the 5 m (17 ft) mark, with an arching, spreading habit. The leaves are three-lobed, 7·5 cm (3 in) long, with the central lobe much longer than the other two. There are small, fragrant bunches of white flowers in May, and a bright red autumn colour.

A. griseum: The paper-bark maple, a 10 m (33 ft) tree with very handsome bark that peels in flakes, revealing the young, orange-red bark underneath. The leaves are formed of three separate toothed leaflets, each about 5 cm (2 in) long, and there is usually a good autumn colour.

A. heldreichii: A very distinctive 12 m (40 ft) tree with 15 cm (6 in) wide, deeply indented five-lobed leaves, .woolly-grey beneath. The broad bunches of yellow flowers in May are followed by the long-winged seeds.

A. henryi: A 7·5 m (25 ft) tree noted for its bunches of red seeds, which are produced in slender racemes. The leaves have three oval leaflets, each 2·5 cm (1 in) wide, and colour well in the autumn.

A. japonicum: This maple sometimes makes a 6 m (20 ft) tree, but is usually grown as a bushy shrub. The leaves have seven or more lobes, and average about 12·5 cm (5 in) long. They always colour brightly in the autumn, and purplish-red flower clusters are produced in the spring. Varieties include 'Aconitifolium', with finely cut leaves that turn brilliantly ruby-crimson in the autumn; 'Aureum' with yellow young leaves; and 'Filicifolium' with very deeply toothed leaves.

A. lobelii: An erect, columnar tree about 15 m (50 ft) high, with bright green five-lobed leaves, each about 15 cm (6 in) wide. As the bark ages it becomes attractively striped.

A. negundo: The box elder, a handsome woodland tree up to 18 m (60 ft) tall, with pinnate ash-like leaves, each leaflet 10–15 cm (4–6 in) long. Varieties include 'Aureum Marginatum', whose leaves have yellow margins; 'Aureum Variegatum', with yellow-blotched leaves; and 'Variegatum', with white-margined leaves.

A. nikoense: A round-topped tree up to 9 m (30 ft). The leaves have three oval leaflets, the middle one 10 cm (4 in) long, the others shorter. There is good autumn colour.

Acer negundo (box elder). This handsome tree has several varieties with variegated leaves.

A. palmatum: May be seen as a small tree up to 6 m (20 ft), but there are many shrubby varieties. Typically, the leaves are five-lobed and deeply indented. As a tree it is most graceful, with bright autumn colours. Some varieties are: 'Dissectum', a dwarf with very deeply cut leaves; 'Dissectum Atropurpureum', with bright crimson leaves; 'Flavescens', variegated cream and yellow; 'Koreanum', with striped bark and brilliant autumn colour; 'Nigrum', with dark purple leaves; 'Ornatum', with deeply cut, bronze-red leaves; 'Lutescens', which yellows in the autumn; and 'Osakazuki', with brilliant orange and scarlet autumn colours.

A. platanoides: Norway maple, a tree of 18 m (60 ft) or more, very rapidly grown, with five-lobed leaves, 15 cm (6 in) wide. There are many varieties, including 'Aureo Variegatum', with yellow margined leaves; 'Drummondii', a very bright variegation of silver-white; 'Schwedleri', whose leaves are red when young, then green, becoming red again for the autumn. Good varieties are often sold under the general description 'purple Norway maple'.

A. pseudoplatanus: European sycamore is a forest tree that can reach a height of 30 m (100 ft). One of the best of all hardwoods for planting in exposed, windy places, it seeds itself readily in the wild, but is not suitable for small gardens. There are several varieties, including: 'Albo Variegatum', with white-marked leaves; 'Atropurpureum', with purple leaves; 'Aureo Variegatum', with yellow blotching; 'Brilliantissimum', a small variety with pink young leaves; 'Leopoldii', with buff-orange leaves; and 'Purpureum', with purple colouring beneath the leaves.

A. rufinerve: This 7 m (23 ft) tree has smooth, dark green bark, marked with paler stripes. The oval or slightly three-lobed leaves have a reddish down on their undersides in the spring, and are about 12·5 cm (5 in) long. There is usually good autumn coloration. Variety 'Albo Limbatum' has leaves that are blotched with white.

A. saccharinum: The silver maple, a large tree up to 24 m (80 ft), with a gracefully drooping habit and a smooth, silver-green bark. The leaves are five-lobed, 10 cm (4 in) long, colouring yellow in the autumn. There are several varieties, including 'Lutescens', whose leaves are a soft yellow throughout the summer; 'Pendulum', with weeping branches, and 'Pyramidale', with upright branches.

Aesculus

The horse chestnuts and the buckeyes. All make very handsome deciduous trees of varying size, and thrive in any soil, acid or limy. Propagation is by seed, and they are sometimes grafted or budded on to horse chestnut seedlings.

A. carnea: The red horse chestnut, a 15 m (50 ft) tree, very like the common white horse chestnut, but with smaller leaves. The flowers are a deep rosy red, or occasionally pale pink. It is of much more manageable proportions for the garden than *A. hippocastanum.* The variety 'Briotii' has larger, brighter red flowers than *A. carnea.*

A. hippocastanum: The white horse chestnut can make a majestic tree up to 30 m (100 ft) tall. It should only be planted where there is park-like space. Lopping the branches, though often practised, is not advisable, as the shortened stumps tend to die back very rapidly and become subject to attack by timber-rotting fungi.

A. indica: The Indian horse chestnut makes a large tree up to 18 m (58 ft), with handsome, glossy foliage and white flowers which are lightly tinged with pink. Like the white horse chestnut it has very sticky winter buds.

A. octandra: The sweet buckeye, a 15 m (50 ft) tree of upright habit, whose smooth bark is marked with distinctive horizontal scars. The leaflets are up to 30 cm (12 in) long and downy on the under surface, and the yellow flowers in erect 15 cm (6 in) panicles appear during May and June.

A. parviflora: A small tree or shrub up to 3 m (10 ft), suckering at the base. The suckers can be removed and planted separately. The leaflets are 15 cm (6 in) long and downy-grey underneath, and the pinky-white flowers appear in August.

A. pavia: The red buckeye, a small tree up to 4 m (13 ft) high, with narrow leaves and bright red flowers in June.

A splendens: A shrub or small tree attaining some 4 m (13 ft), with narrow, 15 cm (6 in) long leaflets. The magnificent long panicles of rich red flowers for which it is noted appear in May.

Ailanthus altissima

The tree of heaven, an unusual deciduous tree up to 15 m (50 ft) tall. It grows very rapidly up to the age of ten years, after which the growth slows down. It may be propagated by root cuttings, and does well in acid or limy soil. It is perhaps better suited for use as a distinctive specimen tree, for example in a lawn setting, rather than actually within woodland.

Alnus

The alders, natives of both Europe and America, are noted for growing well in wet places, and some have been used successfully for planting on slag heaps and similar waste areas. They are not worth introducing into the garden, but where they already exist are invaluable as a light, deciduous canopy to give shade.

Amelanchier

The juneberries, handsome small trees and shrubs, showy when in flower. All are deciduous, and all need a sunny position to give of their best. They may be propagated by seed or layering, and their tolerance to lime in the soil varies from species to species.

A. asiatica: A 6 m (20 ft) tree with graceful, slender branches and downy leaves which develop a striking red autumn coloration. The tree is covered with fragrant white flowers in May, followed by black currant-like fruit. A lime-tolerant species.

A. canadensis: A 6 m (20 ft) tree similar to *asiatica*, but with the white flowers appearing in April, and yellow autumn foliage colour. It prefers a lime-free soil.

A. florida: Another 6 m (20 ft) tree with white flowers appearing in May, but distinguished by its erect branching system. It is tolerant of lime in the soil, and the leaves turn yellow in the autumn.

A. laevis: A tree of similar size and with white flowers in April, but the young leaves are purple at first before becoming green for the summer, then taking on rich red autumn colours. It prefers a lime-free soil.

Aralia elata

The angelica tree, a very striking small tree attaining perhaps 6 m (20 ft), distinguished by its strangely thick twigs and handsome foliage, with compound leaves of a metre (3 ft) long, composed of numerous small leaflets. The white flowers are produced in huge bunches during late summer. A deciduous tree for acid or limy soils, propagated by root cuttings taken in the spring. Varieties include 'Albo Marginata' with creamy-white borders to the leaves, and 'Aureo Variegata' with yellow blotches.

Arbutus unedo

The strawberry tree, a native of southern Europe that is also found growing wild in Ireland, a marvellous evergreen up to 9 m (30 ft) tall. It thrives on limy soils, but also does well on acid sites provided the soil is deep and well drained. The clusters of white flowers start to appear in late summer, forming strawberry-like fruits in October. Very useful for planting in exposed places and by the coast. Propagation is by seed, or by cuttings of soft shoots taken in the summer.

Betula

The birches are handsome and very hardy trees. The silver bark of European and American species is well known as a valuable foil to

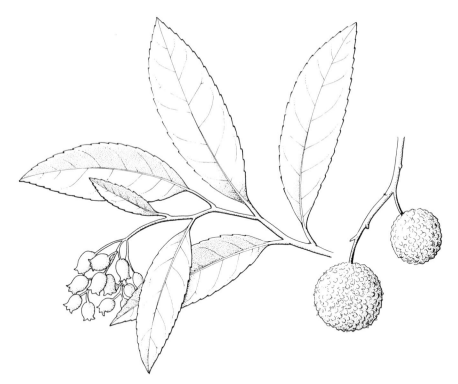

Arbutus unedo (strawberry tree). White flower clusters appear in late summer, followed by strawberry-like fruits in October.

almost any plant, and as a contrast with dark-foliaged shrubs, while some Asian birches have highly ornamental bark of colours other than white. Birches are deciduous, light-demanding trees and will not grow in shade, and because of their own lightly dappled shade, they are the ideal trees under which to plant woodland shrubs. They grow well on any soil, and are propagated by seed, the varieties being grafted onto seedling stocks.

B. albo-sinensis: A tall tree—up to 23 m (77 ft)—noted for its bright orange-red peeling bark.

B. japonica: A 15 m (50 ft) tree with pure white bark. Varieties, which some hold to be closely related species, are: 'Manshurica', with larger leaves, and 'Szechuanica', with extra long catkins and the purest white bark of any birch.

B. maximowiczii: A tall tree of 23 m (77 ft) or more, with a grey or orangey bark, and noted for the size of its leaves, which may be up to 15 cm (6 in) long.

B. papyrifera: The canoe birch of Canada and Alaska, an 18 m (60 ft) tree, with pure white bark and a slender, graceful habit. Variety 'Occidentalis' attains nearly 40 m (133 ft) in the wild, and is the largest of all the birches.

B. pendula: The silver birch of Europe and Britain, a 15 m (50 ft) tree of graceful, weeping habit, with silvery-white peeling bark which becomes dark and rough at the base. The young shoots are smooth. Varieties include 'Dalecarlica' the Swedish birch, with deeply lobed leaves; 'Purpurea' with purple leaves; and 'Youngii', Young's weeping birch, which has a very pendulous habit with no distinct leading shoot, and is usually grafted onto an upright stem.

B. pubescens: The white birch of Europe and Britain, a 15 m (50 ft) tree with white, peeling bark, reddish when young but becoming dark and rough at the base with age. The young shoots are downy. Varieties include 'Aurea' with yellow young leaves, and 'Crenata Nana', a dwarf bush.

Carpinus betulus

The hornbeam, a hardy tree up to 25 m (83 ft) tall, somewhat similar in general appearance to beech, but the seed has a distinctive three-lobed wing. It will grow in any soil, and is propagated by seed. Like beech, it may be used as a deciduous hedge plant. Varieties include 'Asplenifolia', the fern-leaved hornbeam; 'Columnaris', which makes a splendid spire; 'Pendula', an elegant weeping form; 'Purpurea', with purple young leaves, and 'Pyramidalis', with erect-growing branches.

Catalpa bignonioides

A beautiful, spreading, deciduous 12 m (40 ft) tree with striking 20 cm (8 in) long leaves of a restful, pale green. The flowers which appear in July are yellow and white with purple markings, in erect panicles over 20 cm (8 in) across. Later, the tree becomes festooned with 30 cm (12 in) long pods. It likes a good, deep, moist soil, but will grow whether there is lime or not. Its shape makes it a perfect foil to stand next to tall, spire-like trees such as the pyramidal conifers. It is propagated by seed, or by cuttings taken of side shoots in the late summer and kept shaded in a heated frame. *Catalpa* really needs a large garden, but is well worth the space it takes up. Variety 'Aurea' is a beautiful tree with yellow leaves.

Cedrus

The cedars eventually make very large trees, but there are dwarf and slow-growing forms that are suitable for the smaller garden. All are coniferous and evergreen, and they grow well in all soil types. Propagation of the species is by seed, but the garden varieties need to be grafted on seedling stocks.

C. atlantica: The Atlantic cedar has green or slightly grey-green leaves, and branches that tend to ascend from the main stem. The species makes an erect tree of 36 m (120 ft), but the most popular variety is 'Glauca', the very beautiful blue cedar which reaches 30 m (100 ft). There is also 'Glauca Pendula', which makes a small and striking specimen tree of some 6 m (20 ft), but it needs a site of its own, and is out of place in the woodland.

C. deodara: The deodar, a very graceful 45 m (150 ft) tree with somewhat weeping branches and a leading shoot which also droops. The leaves are grey-green at first, becoming dark green.

C. libani: The Lebanon cedar, a 24 m (80 ft) tree which spreads widely as it matures, the heavy branches becoming horizontally tiered and the crown flat-topped. The leaves are usually dark green.

Cercis siliquastrum

The Judas tree, a very attractive deciduous tree attaining 9 m (30 ft) eventually, with grey-green, heart-shaped leaves. It becomes absolutely covered with rose-purple pea-flowers in May, and later in the year by 10 cm (4 in) long pods with purple markings. The crown of this beautiful tree needs the sun, but is ideal for underplanting with shrubs as the shade it casts is light, and the roots are well behaved. It may be propagated by seed. There is a variety called 'Bodnant' which has darker purple flowers.

Cercis siliquastrum (judas tree). The numerous rose-purple pea-flowers in spring are followed by purple pods (inset).

Chamaecyparis lawsoniana

Lawson's cypress has numerous varieties suitable for the garden. Some are dwarf or very slow growing and thus especially suitable for the rock garden. The typical species makes a handsome evergreen forest tree which may attain 25 m (83 ft), and thrives in all types of soil. It is propagated by seed, but the varieties should be grown from cuttings taken in June. Usually they root very readily, but the degree of success does seem to vary. When young, the leaves have a distinct, prickly appearance, and in some varieties the tree retains this juvenile foliage into maturity.

Cornus

The cornels or dogwoods are best known as shrubs, and are often coppiced to make the most of their decorative bark. The best trees of this genus, all of which are deciduous, are:

C. controversa: A tree up to 9 m (30 ft), with flat, horizontal tiers of branches, 15 cm (6 in) long leaves coloured dark glossy green on their upper surfaces and grey beneath, and clusters of cream-coloured flowers produced in June and July, followed by blue-black berries. This fine tree thrives in acid or limy soils, and is propagated by seed or layers.

C. florida: A small tree—4·5 m (15 ft) high—called the flowering dogwood on account of the large and showy white bracts which appear in May. It tolerates lime, but not shallow chalk soils. Propagation may be by seed or layering.

C. kousa: A tree up to 6 m (20 ft), with elegant, spreading branches and creamy white flower bracts in June. It tolerates lime, but is not successful on shallow chalk soils. Propagated by layers and seed.

C. macrophylla: A tree up to 12 m (40 ft), with long leaves that are dark glossy green above and downy-grey beneath. The yellowish-white flowers in 15 cm (6 in) panicles appear in July and August, followed by the blue-black berries in autumn. It tolerates a limy soil. Propagation is normally by layers.

C. mas: The cornelian cherry, usually seen as a large, spreading shrub, but may be trained as a small tree up to 7·5 m (25 ft) tall. The rather showy yellow flowers are produced before the leaves appear in early spring, and the bright red berries which follow are edible. The species is tolerant of lime, and is usually propagated by seed or layers. Varieties include 'Aurea', which has yellow leaves; 'Aurea Elegantissima', which is tinted yellow and pink; and 'Variegata', which is variegated with silver.

C. nuttallii: In British gardens makes a tree up to 6 m (20 ft), but in North America where it is at home it reaches large forest tree

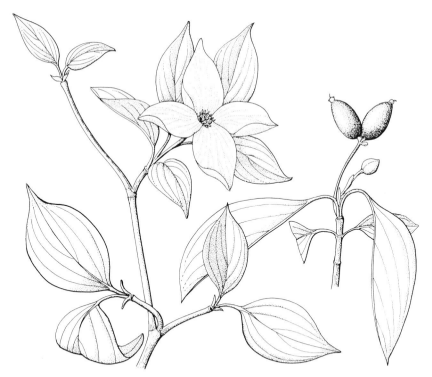

Cornus florida (flowering dogwood). Flowers and fruits. The large flower 'petals' are really bracts.

size. It tolerates lime, but is not successful on shallow soils over chalk. This is a handsome tree, flowering in May with large creamy-white bracts that are flushed with pink, and foliage that colours well in the autumn.

Cotinus coggygria

The smoke tree is so-called on account of the clouds of plume-like flowerheads appearing in June and July. It makes an extremely ornamental 3 m (10 ft) tree, picturesquely branched, thriving in most soils and situations. The rounded green leaves colour strongly in the autumn, but the varieties 'Foliis Purpureis' and 'Royal Purple' have richly coloured leaves throughout the summer, and both make really beautiful little trees. The usual method of propagation is by mound layering: a strong shoot must be pegged down in the spring, horizontally, 2–3 cm (1 in) above the ground. When young shoots appear and start to grow verti-cally, soil is heaped over the layer, leaving only the tips of the new shoots showing. This is repeated every two weeks until the shoots are covered to a depth of 15 cm (6 in). In the autumn, the base of the layered branch is partially severed, and rooting below each of the shoots should have taken place by the following spring, when they can be lifted and separated.

Cotoneaster frigida

One of the few cotoneasters that attain tree size—up to 10 m (33 ft) or more—this is ideal as a low over-storey shade tree. It thrives in acid or limy soil, and always produces a good show of red berries which are normally used for propagation, though the varieties which follow must be grafted: 'Fructo Luteo' has yellow berries; 'Pendula' has a weeping habit and makes a charming small tree, virtually limited in height to the stem on which it has been grafted.

Crataegus

The hawthorns, well known deciduous trees that are tolerant of all kinds of soils and situations. The species are propagated by seed, but the varieties are budded or grafted onto seedling stocks. After sowing, the seed is apt to lie dormant for eighteen months, and to avoid this it should be stratified or stored in boxes of moist sand until the second spring, when the seeds and sand are sown together, with excellent results.

C. monogyna: The common thorn, a tree up to 10 m (33 ft) tall. Varieties include: 'Aurea', with yellow berries; 'Lutescens', with yellow leaves; 'Praecox' is the Glastonbury thorn of legend, which flowers in the winter and comes into leaf very early in the year.

C. oxyacantha: A similar hawthorn, but smaller and less thorny, reaching a height of about 4 m (13 ft). It is the parent species of most of our showy garden varieties: 'Alba Plena', with double white flowers; 'Candida Plena', with double flowers of a purer white; 'Coccinea', scarlet; 'Coccinea Plena', known as Paul's double scarlet; 'Fructu Lutea', with yellow berries; 'Gireoudii', with pinky-white blossom; 'Maskei', double pale pink; 'Rosea', single pink; and 'Salisburifolia', a dwarf variety with double red flowers.

C. prunifolia: A fine tree up to 6 m (20 ft), with very large bright green leaves and clusters of pinkish-white flowers in June, followed by large, richly red berries. It also colours well in the autumn.

Cryptomeria japonica

The Japanese cedar is a very ornamental, fast-growing conifer which makes a large forest tree exceeding 20 m (65 ft). It grows well in most types of soil, and is propagated by seed or by cuttings taken in early autumn. There are several varieties, mainly dwarf and slow-growing kinds suitable for the rock garden.

34

× Cupressocyparis leylandii

Well known as the fastest-growing evergreen conifer in Britain, the leyland cypress is usually planted when a rapid screen or tall-growing hedge is required. It grows well on all types of soil and there are several varieties, varying in leaf colour and density of growth. It is quite easily propagated from cuttings. When grown as an isolated specimen tree, leyland cypress will attain some 24 m (80 ft).

Cupressus macrocarpa

Monterey cypress is a fast-growing 18 m (60 ft) conifer of some-what spreading habit, with bright green leaf sprays. It is usually propagated from seed, but there are several varieties suitable for the rock garden, and these must be grafted.

Davidia involucrata

A 10 m (33 ft) woodland tree with ornately ascending branches and a well-balanced shape. The leaves resemble those of a lime, but the distinctive large white flower bracts which appear in May make the tree very showy, and these are followed by plum-like fruits. This hardy deciduous tree thrives in acid or limy soils, and is propagated by means of short side-shoot cuttings taken during the summer.

Davidia involucrata. A hardy deciduous tree which thrives in acid or limy soils.

Eucalyptus

The gum trees of Australasia, beautiful broadleaf evergreens with ornamental bark and leathery foliage, often scented. They grow very rapidly, and are not usually fussy in their soil requirements, though they dislike shallow soils over chalk. *E. parvifolia* is an exception which seems to do well in this situation. It is a vast genus, and the great majority of the species need a sub-tropical climate. Their size varies in a temperate climate, but they may eventually surpass 12 m (40 ft). They are propagated by sowing imported seed. Those which thrive in temperate conditions include:

E. camphora: A small tree which prefers moist sites; it has attractive globular white flowers, glaucous leaves and a distinctive, rough bark.

E. dalrympleana: Makes a larger tree with a very attractive bark, pitted and dappled in shades of green and white. The leaves are bronze-coloured at first, becoming glaucous-green as they mature.

E. gunnii: Quite a large tree, with mottled grey-green bark, and white flowers which appear in the autumn. The leaves are rounded and blue-grey when young, later becoming long, narrow, curved and green.

E. johnstonii: A small tree, with peeling, reddish-brown bark and bright green leaves.

E. niphophila: The snow gum, a mountain species whose distinctive bark is dappled grey, green and cream; it bears large, glaucous-green leaves.

E. parvifolia: A very hardy, medium-sized gum tree which does well in limy soils and chalk. The young leaves are rounded, becoming narrow, pointed and glaucous-green as they mature.

Fagus sylvatica

The beech; one of the noblest of forest hardwoods, up to 30 m (100 ft) high. Its numbers have been seriously depleted by bark disease, which is an infection spread by insects, and which strikes hardest after the trees have been weakened by a summer of drought. It is a difficult tree to garden under as the shade is so dense, and the roots are largely surface feeding; where beech trees exist as an over-storey, heavy crown thinning is usually necessary before underplanting can take place. Beech is extremely shade-tolerant when young and, because of this, it is often introduced into existing woodland by underplanting. These deciduous trees thrive in any good, deep soil, and are propagated by seed, except for named varieties which have to be grafted. A very small proportion of copper beech appear in batches of normal seedlings, however.

Varieties include: 'Cuprea', the copper beech; 'Fastigiata', the Dawyck beech, a narrowly pyramidal form; 'Heterophylla', the fern-leaved beech; 'Pendula', the weeping beech, with long branch-lets hanging down to the ground; 'Purple Dawyck', a small, nar-rowly pyramidal purple-leaved tree; 'Purpurea', the purple beech, a very handsome tree, but there are several forms varying in the intensity of their purple colour.

Fraxinus

The ash trees are divided into two groups: the large and the small flowered. All are deciduous, light-demanding trees which cast comparatively little shade and so are ideal for planting under. They prefer limestone soils, but thrive in most sites. The species are propagated from seed, but the varieties must be grafted.

F. bungeana: A small tree seldom exceeding 5 m (16 ft), with dainty foliage and pleasant white flowers appearing in May.

F. excelsior: The British ash, a very large tree reaching 40 m (133 ft) in height. Where a grove of ash already exists, this is an ideal basis for a woodland garden. The best specimens are grown on heavy, calcareous loams, but as an ornamental tree it will do well on any soil. An attractive variety for the garden is 'Pendula', the weeping ash.

F. mariesii: A handsome tree up to 7 m (23 ft) tall, with creamy-white panicles of flower in June and distinctive purple seed-keys.

F. ornus: Manna ash makes an 18 m (60 ft) tree, similar in appearance to the British ash, but with bunches of fragrant white flowers in May. It casts perhaps rather more shade than *excelsior*.

Ginkgo biloba

The maidenhair tree, a distinctive deciduous conifer, with fan-shaped leaves and yellow plum-like fruits which give off an offen-sive smell when they fall in the autumn—for this reason, male plants are usually chosen for garden use. The leaves turn yellow before they fall. Maidenhair will grow in most soils, is tolerant of smoky industrial conditions and will sometimes exceed 30 m (100 ft). Propagation is normally by seed.

Gleditschia

Elegant deciduous trees similar to the mimosas in their fern-like foliage and large pods. They grow well in all types of loamy soil, and colour brightly in the autumn. Propagation is by seed.

G. delavayi: A tree up to 15 m (50 ft) tall, with fiercely spiny twigs, and dark green leaves which are coppery-red in spring.

G. japonica: A graceful, cone-shaped 15 m (50 ft) tree, with a spiny trunk and curiously twisted, 30 cm (12 in) long pods.

G. triacanthos: The honey locust, so called because the 45 cm (18 in) long pods are packed with a sweet, sticky substance. It makes a handsome 20 m (66 ft) tree. There are varieties of honey locust which are shrubs, but the popular 'Sunburst' makes a medium-sized tree, without thorns, very attractive in the spring when the foliage is bright yellow.

Halesia

The snowdrop trees like a lime-free soil that is sandy and moist. They are all deciduous, and are propagated from seed, or by layering in early spring just as the buds are opening.

H. carolina: A small tree up to 6 m (20 ft) tall—or a large shrub—covered with clusters of white snowdrop-like flowers in May.

H. diptera: A small tree up to 3 m (10 ft) tall, with broader leaves than *carolina*, but with similar white flowers in the spring.

H. monticola: Makes a tree up to 18 m (60 ft), with high-spreading branches and flaky bark; very showy when the white flower clusters appear in May. The variety 'Rosea' has pink flowers.

Juglans

The walnuts, handsome deciduous trees which like a good, loamy soil, either acid or limy. They are propagated from seed.

J. nigra: The black walnut, a fast-growing tree up to 23 m (77 ft) tall, with large leaves and a deeply furrowed bark. The fruits are usually in pairs.

J. regia: The common walnut also makes a fine tree to 23 m (77 ft), with a large dome-shaped crown. It is valued for its nuts.

Juniperus virginiana

A medium-sized evergreen conifer with a broadly conical outline. The leaves are of two types, often appearing together on the same spray: the green, sharply scale-like adult foliage, and the glaucous-grey, prickly juvenile leaves. A very hardy tree that will grow in all soils and situations, it is propagated either by seed or by cuttings of shoot-tips taken in summer or autumn. There are many garden varieties, most of which are dwarf forms suitable for the rock garden.

Koelreuteria paniculata

A very handsome, wide-spreading deciduous tree up to 10 m (33 ft), which thrives in acid or limy soils. The large, many-flowered panicles of bright yellow flowers appear in July, and are followed by showy three-lobed fruit. It may be propagated by seed or root cuttings.

Laburnum

Well known small deciduous ornamentals sometimes called golden chain trees. They thrive in all types of soil, and may be grown either from seed or by 25 cm (10 in) long cuttings taken in the autumn.

L. alpinum: The Scotch laburnum is especially attractive in the small garden, for it seldom exceeds 4·5 m (15 ft) and the mode of growth is often gnarled and picturesque, like a Japanese bonsai tree. The fragrant yellow flowers appear in early June.

L. anagyroides: The common laburnum attains 7–8 m (23–26 ft), flowers in May, and often seeds itself very readily. A good variety is 'Vossii', a free-flowering form with very long racemes of the familiar yellow flowers, and a type which seldom produces seed —an advantage where children are around, because laburnum seeds are poisonous.

Laburnocytisus × adami

A hybrid which arose by accident when the purple-flowered *Cytisus purpureus* was grafted onto a laburnum stock. As a result, one plant grew inside the other and produced a small tree whose appearance is variable between the two parents. The foliage is similar to laburnum, but the flowers may be purple broom on some branches, yellow laburnum on others, while an intermediate type may appear at the same time. An interesting freak which grows in most soils and situations, but not a particularly attractive tree. For propagation, the original graft is usually repeated, but it will root from 20 cm (8 in) long cuttings taken in the autumn and set out over winter in sandy soil.

Larix

The larches, deciduous forest conifers that may attain 45 m (150 ft) or more. They cast very light shade, and for this reason a grove of larch forms an ideal basis for a woodland garden. They will grow well in most soil types, and propagation is by seed.

L. decidua: The European larch, a handsome and valuable tree with light green leaves and yellowish shoots.

L. × eurolepis: The Dunkeld larch, a hybrid between the European and the Japanese larches, a very vigorous tree with slightly glaucous foliage and buff-coloured shoots.

L. kaempferi: The Japanese larch, of vigorous and rapid growth, with darkish green leaves and distinctly reddish shoots which in winter give groups of the tree a purple, hazy appearance.

Libocedrus decurrens

The incense cedar, a tall, columnar, coniferous evergreen with arching, fan-like sprays of dark green foliage. It will grow well in all types of soil, and is excellent by reason of its characteristic shape to plant in association with low, spreading hardwoods—a combination that cannot fail to impress. Mature specimens may exceed 33 m (110 ft). Propagation is by seed where this is available, otherwise cuttings of shoot tips may be taken in August and struck in a closed frame.

Liquidambar styraciflua

A deciduous maple-like tree up to 18 m (60 ft), with a corky grey bark and ornate five- or seven-lobed leaves which colour beautifully in the autumn. It dislikes limy soil. It is propagated by seed, or by layers which root very quickly.

Liriodendron tulipifera

The tulip tree, a handsome, fast-growing deciduous tree up to 30 m (100 ft) tall, will grow in any reasonably good soil. It has very distinctively shaped leaves which turn yellow in the autumn, and unusual tulip-shaped flowers of greenish-yellow, marked inside the cups with orange, and which appear in June and July. Propagation is normally by seed, but only a small percentage will prove fertile.

Magnolia

Some of the most magnificent flowering trees are included in this genus, and many are bushy shrubs. All like a reasonably good, deep soil, and flourish in heavy clay, but they vary in their tolerance of lime. The early spring-flowering kinds may be subject to frost damage of their flowers. They may be propagated by seed which should be sown as soon as it is ripe in peaty beds, or they may be layered in the spring. In the latter case, rooting is accelerated if an extra long cut of about 5 cm (2 in) is made upwards through a bud, before pegging the shoot down firmly.

M. acuminata: A vigorous, tall tree—up to 25 m (83 ft)—deciduous and very tolerant of limy soil. The flowers appear from May to July, are greenish-yellow, and are not produced by very young plants.

M. ashei: A shrubby tree up to 15 m (50 ft) tall, deciduous and lime-hating. The flowers, which are produced while the plant is

Liriodendron tulipifera (tulip tree). The tulip-shaped flowers which are borne in June or July are greenish-yellow, marked with orange.

still young, are large and fragrant, white with purple markings, and appear in the spring at the same time as the leaves.

M. campbellii: A 20 m (67 ft) deciduous tree which will not stand lime. The large flowers which appear in February and March are deep pink on the outside and light pink inside. Young trees do not flower, but old trees are spectacular. There are several splendid varieties, mainly with larger, darker flowers, but there is also a white-flowered form.

M. cordata: A round-headed tree to 10 m (33 ft), with soft yellow flowers in late summer and early autumn. Lime tolerant and deciduous.

M. denudata: A deciduous, lime-hating small tree attaining some 7·5 m (24½ ft), with a compact, rounded shape. The fragrant, pure white flowers appear before the leaves in early spring. There is a shrubby, spreading variety called 'Purple Eye', which has a purple spot at the base of each petal.

M. grandiflora: A spectacular evergreen, often grown as a wall plant, but which makes a magnificent tree up to 24 m (80 ft) when planted in a sunny position in the open. It is lime tolerant in a good soil. The leaves are large, leathery, and a dark glossy green. The huge, fragrant, creamy-white flowers appear in the summer and early autumn. There are several varieties, among them 'Exmouth' and 'Goliath', both of which have larger flowers which open earlier in the summer.

M. kobus: A deciduous tree up to 6 m (20 ft) tall, tolerant of lime. It produces creamy-white flowers in April and May, but very young plants do not flower.

M. liliflora: Usually takes a shrubby form up to 4 m (13 ft) high, deciduous and lime-hating. The flowers are large and bell-shaped, purple outside and creamy-white inside, appearing from April to June. The variety 'Nigra' has larger flowers more deeply stained purple.

M. macrophylla: A deciduous, lime-hating small tree seldom exceeding 10 m (33 ft) in height, with an open, spreading habit. It has larger leaves and flowers than any other magnolia. The huge flowers are fragrant and creamy-white, purple at the base, appearing in May and June.

M. salicifolia: A 10 m (33 ft) tree with narrow, willow-like leaves, deciduous and lime-hating, with fragrant white flowers appearing just before the leaves unfurl in April.

M. sargentiana: Makes a comparatively large tree, up to 15 m

Magnolia grandiflora. The glossy, dark green leaves and large creamy-white flowers make this a spectacular tree.

(50 ft) tall, deciduous and lime-hating, with leathery, grey-green leaves, and bowl-shaped flowers of rose pink which appear in April, just before the leaves open.

M. sieboldii: A small tree up to 3 m (10 ft), or sometimes a bushy shrub. The dark green leaves are downy grey underneath, and the fragrant, creamy-white flowers appear from May to August. The fruits in crimson clusters are also very showy. Deciduous and lime tolerant, this is one of the best woodland magnolias whose flowers cannot suffer from frost damage.

M. sinensis: Makes a small tree up to 6 m (20 ft) but is often grown as a large shrub. Deciduous, lime tolerant, with rounded leaves and nodding, lemon-scented white flowers which appear in June.

M.× soulangeana: A multi-stemmed spreading shrub attaining 7·5 m (24½ ft), deciduous and lime tolerant, with huge tulip-shaped flowers—white with purple staining at the base of each petal—produced in April and May. There are many varieties, one of the best of which is 'Lennei', which has larger leaves, and flowers which are purple inside and out.

M. sprengeri: A deciduous, lime-hating tree up to 10 m (33 ft), with very large, fragrant, rose pink flowers in April.

M. stellata: A compactly shaped, thickly branched shrub up to 3 m (10 ft) tall, deciduous and lime tolerant, with fragrant white flowers appearing in March and April before the leaves unfurl. So early in the season, they are apt to be damaged by frost, but as they open successively and in great profusion, many of them usually escape damage. There is a variety 'Rosea' which has pink flowers.

M. wilsonii: A tree up to 10 m (33 ft), or sometimes a wide-spreading shrub, deciduous and lime tolerant, with somewhat narrow, pointed leaves which are brownish on their undersurface. The nodding, white, cup-shaped flowers with conspicuous crimson stamens are produced in May and June, followed by showy purplish-pink fruits. It enjoys light shade.

Malus

The flowering crab apples; small deciduous trees which grow well in all types of soil, and all very beautiful when in flower. Some of them also have showy fruits. The true species may be propagated from seed, but named varieties need to be budded or grafted in the same way as orchard apples.

M. × aldenhamensis: The young leaves are purple at first, becoming bronze-green during the summer. Deep wine-red flowers appear in May, to be followed by reddish fruits. Maximum height is 4 m (13 ft).

M. baccata: Makes a round-headed tree up to 10–11 m (33–37 ft) tall, with white flowers in May, followed by red or yellow berries.

M. 'Crittenden': A small, compact tree with pale pink blossom, and a profusion of bright red fruits which persist over winter. Height is approximately 8 m (26 ft).

M. 'Echtermeyer': A low, wide-spreading little tree with gracefully pendulous branches, bronzy-purple leaves, rose-crimson flowers, and reddish-purple fruits. Height is about 4 m (13 ft).

M. floribunda: The Japanese crab, a small tree attaining some 7·5 m (24½ ft), with wide-spreading, arching branches. One of the earliest of the genus to flower, crimson in the bud, opening to palest pink. The fruits are small, red and yellow.

M. 'Golden Hornet': A small tree with white flowers and a heavy crop of bright yellow crab apples which last on the tree well during the winter. Maximum height is about 6 m (20 ft).

M. hupehensis: An upright-growing tree as tall as 10 m (33 ft), with fragrant white flowers—pink in the bud—produced in great abundance during May and June. The fruits are yellow with red cheeks. There is a variety 'Rosea' with pale pink flowers and a more spreading habit.

M. 'John Downie': Often said to be the best fruiting crab of all, the white flowers are followed by masses of bright orange and scarlet fruits of good flavour. About 8 m (26 ft).

M. 'Katherine': A small tree with an even, round head. The very fragrant, large and semi-double pink flowers are followed by bright red and yellow fruits. Height about 5 m (16 ft).

M. 'Lady Northcliffe': A small tree with a dense, spreading crown. The blossom is a deep carmine when in bud, opening pink, and finally becoming white. The fruits are small and yellow. Maximum height is 5 m (16 ft).

M. 'Profusion': A small tree with coppery-red leaves, and profuse, fragrant, wine-red blossom. The fruits are small and red. It should not exceed 3 m (10 ft).

M. tschonoskii: Makes a 10 m (33 ft) tree with a conical, upright habit. It has pinkish-white flowers and purplish-yellow fruits, but is mainly planted for its fiery autumn foliage colours.

Metasequoia glyptostroboides

The dawn redwood, a tree which was not discovered in other than fossil form until the 1940s in China. It is a deciduous conifer with shaggy brown bark and bright green, feathery leaves which colour pink and yellow before falling in the autumn. It thrives vigorously in all types of soil, though it is probably less healthy on chalk. It is propagated from seed. Mature specimens will attain 20 m (67 ft).

Morus nigra

The mulberry makes a 7–8 m (23–26 ft) tree with a picturesque, rugged manner of growth. It has large, heart-shaped leaves and pleasantly tasting, dark red fruit. A deciduous tree, the hardiest of its genus, which succeeds on any reasonable soil. It may be propagated by cuttings of side-shoots taken in the summer, or alternatively by 25–30 cm (10–12 in) hardwood cuttings taken in the autumn and set in the open.

Nothofagus

The southern beeches, large trees similar in general appearance to the European beech. They need an acid soil to do well, and do not appreciate exposure to high winds, but some of them are useful as rapidly grown plantation trees.

N. antarctica: A fast-growing, bushy, deciduous tree up to 30 m (100 ft) tall, with distinctive small leaves and bright yellow autumn colour. It is propagated by layering in the autumn.

N. dombeyi: A vigorous evergreen tree to 25 m (84 ft), hardy in less extreme areas, but it may lose its leaves during hard winters. With its dark green, shining leaves and glossy, rich brown bark it makes a very handsome specimen. It may be propagated by side-shoot cuttings taken in July.

N. procera: A fast-growing 25 m (84 ft) tree similar in general appearance to the hornbeam, with an erect, stiffly-branched habit of growth. A deciduous tree which is propagated by side-shoot cuttings in the early summer.

Nyssa sylvatica

A handsome, slow-growing deciduous tree attaining 25 m (83 ft), densely branched and with a broadly columnar outline; noted for its fiery autumn colours. It requires a moist soil that is free from lime, and is normally grown from seed that has been imported.

Parrotia persica

A small, wide-spreading, deciduous tree about 9 m (30 ft) tall, thriving in any soil type. A woodland species that assumes magnificent autumn colours. Both the foliage and the peeling, grey-mottled bark are very ornamental, and in outline it complements perfectly those trees which are of tall, columnar growth. Propagated by layering in the spring.

Paulownia

Wonderful small flowering trees with huge, deciduous, heart-shaped leaves, and erect panicles of foxglove-like flowers which

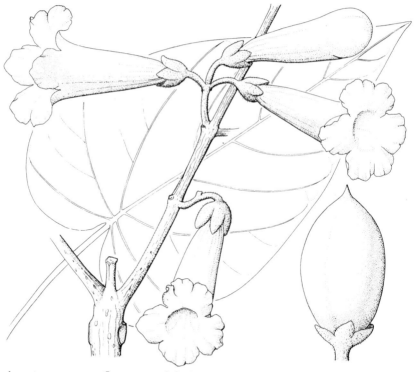

Paulownia tomentosa, flowers and fruit.

are formed in the autumn, but do not open until spring. Although thriving in any soil, they need careful placing as their crowns seek the sun, but a dark background is desirable for the flowers to be seen at their best. They are normally grown from seed; alternatively, root cuttings may be taken in December, cut into short lengths and potted singly.

P. fargesii: The largest of the genus, sometimes reaching 20 m (67 ft), with pale purple flowers and soft, downy leaves. It is perfectly hardy, and less likely than the closely related *P. tomentosa* to lose its flower buds after spring frosts.

P. tomentosa: A similar tree to *P. fargesii*, but with darker flowers that open in May, and so are sometimes liable to damage by late frosts. Mature specimens average 10 m (33 ft), but instead of growing in tree form, young plants may be cut back to ground level in the spring and allowed to coppice for the sake of their huge, sculptural leaves. Young plants, however, do not normally flower.

Photinia villosa

A deciduous little broad-crowned tree, rarely exceeding 5 m (16 ft), with hawthorn-like flowers in May, followed by bright red berries. It does not do well on limy soils. Propagate from seed, layers, side-shoot cuttings in the summer or autumn cuttings.

Picea

The spruces, coniferous evergreens which thrive in most soils. They are usually large, highly decorative trees, splendid for forming small groups in large gardens, but not altogether suitable for planting beneath, as they cast a heavy shade and are near-surface rooting. There are numerous dwarf and slow-growing varieties suitable for the rock garden, and normally these must be propagated by grafting. The true species, however, are all grown from seed.

P. abies: The Norway spruce, commonly grown for use as a Christmas tree, eventually forms a handsome tree up to 50 m (166 ft) tall, with compact, bright green foliage.

P. brewerana: The weeping spruce, one of the most beautiful of all conifers, a 25 m (83 ft) tree whose wide-spreading branches droop at the ends in long, graceful fronds.

P. omorika: The Serbian spruce, a tall, graceful, slender tree up to 30 m (100 ft), with branches that curve upwards at their tips. The best spruce to plant in chalky soils, and in smoky industrial areas.

P. pungens glauca: The Colorado spruce, a conical tree up to 25 m (83 ft) tall, with distinctively dense, prickly, glaucous-blue foliage.

P. sitchensis: The Sitka spruce, a valuable and extremely hardy 50 m (166 ft) forest tree that is often planted on exposed moorland sites. It has prickly, glaucous leaves.

Pinus

The pines, a very large genus of coniferous evergreens, many of which have been planted to good effect in the garden. Scots pine is one of the best for the ornamental woodland, and most are used in forestry, those species whose needles are in sets of two being as a rule the hardiest. None of the pines will stand shade for long, and as they cast comparatively little shade themselves, they are useful for planting under. They are all grown from seed.

P. contorta: Lodgepole pine, a vigorous, hardy species of variable size usually about 10 m (33 ft), often used for planting in poor, dry soil and sand dunes. However, it will not tolerate lime. The leaves are in pairs, very light green in colour, and showing the characteristic twist that gives the species its name.

P. nigra austriaca: The Austrian pine makes a hefty tree up to 45 m (150 ft), with dark, rough bark and dark green leaves in pairs. It grows well in all sorts of situations, including chalk soils and by the sea.

P. nigra calabrica: The Corsican pine is of a similar size, but has lighter bark and grey-green leaves, and casts considerably less shade than the Austrian pine. It grows well in almost any soil or situation, limy or acid, and is used extensively in forestry.

P. radiata: Monterey pine prefers mild districts, and is not fond of limy soils. It grows fairly rapidly up to 35 m (117 ft) or so, but when young is slenderly conical. The bright, dark green needles which are arranged in threes give the tree an attractive, healthy appearance.

P. strobus: Weymouth pine, a very resinous tree with grey-green leaves in fives, of neatly conical shape when young, eventually reaching 30 m (100 ft). It does not like limy soils, but grows rapidly on sandy loams.

P. sylvestris: Scots pine, a native British tree that does well on almost any site. It is also one of the most beautiful of pines, with its characteristically orange young bark, and bluish-green leaves in pairs. Old trees, which may attain 30 m (100 ft), become rounded in the crown. There are several dwarf-growing garden varieties.

Platanus

The planes are very like the maples with their ornamental, flaking bark and lobed leaves. They will grow well in all soils and situa-

Pinus sylvestris (Scots pine). Considered to be one of the most beautiful of all the pines. This drawing shows a mature cone which has shed its seed.

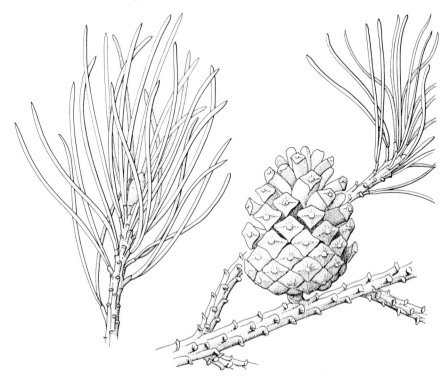

tions, but are said not to attain their full size in limy soils, and to dislike shallow soils overlying chalk.

P. × hispanica: The London plane, a hybrid up to 30 m (100 ft) tall, which is not found in the wild. It is planted extensively as a street tree on account of its great hardiness and tolerance of atmospheric pollution and heavy pruning and, of course, its extremely handsome appearance. A deciduous tree, it is propagated from 25 cm (10 in) cuttings taken in the autumn and lined out in open ground.

P. orientalis: A large deciduous tree, sometimes 30 m (100 ft) tall, with wide-spreading crown, attractively dappled bark, lobed leaves and bristly clusters of fruit like those of the London plane. Splendid as a park tree, but too big for the average garden. Propagated by layering in the spring.

Populus

There are numerous species and varieties of poplar, many of them valuable as timber trees. Most are very fast growing with greedy root systems, and they are usually out of place in the garden. In cases where a really large and rapid screen is needed however, the Lombardy poplar *P. nigra italica* is of great value. Most of the poplars may be used to form a temporary shade-cover while slower growing trees are given the chance to develop their crowns, but when this is done it is essential to remove them before they become large enough to cause trouble with their roots. They are readily propagated from 20–25 cm (8–10 in) cuttings taken in the autumn and set out in open ground. Most poplars will exceed 20 m (100 ft).

Prunus

This enormous genus includes many of our finest flowering trees, and all are extremely tolerant of varied soils and situations. The Japanese flowering cherries cast a fairly heavy shade in mid-summer, and their roots tend to feed near the surface; in the case of larger trees, it is often as well to 'raise the crowns' as far as possible. Most of the species and varieties are propagated by grafting or budding onto seedling wild cherries. All those listed here are deciduous.

P. 'Accolade': An 8 m (26 ft) cherry tree of spreading habit, with pendulous clusters of semi-double, deep pink flowers in the early spring.

P. × amygdalo-persica 'Pollardii': The finest flowering almond hybrid, a 7·5 m (24½ ft) tree which thrives in industrial areas. The beautiful deep pink flowers are produced very early in the year.

P. avium: The wild cherry or gean, a 15 m (50 ft) British wood-land tree with an attractive reddish-brown and grey peeling bark. The clustered white flowers appear in April and May, and the leaves colour well in the autumn. There is a lovely double-flowered variety 'Plena'.

P. cerasifera: The myrobalan, a tree up to 9–10 m (30–33 ft) that becomes covered with tiny white flowers during March. It also makes a good hedging plant. There are several choice varieties, including: 'Nigra', with very dark purple leaves and stems, and pink flowers during March and April; 'Pissardii', with dark red young leaves and shoots which become deep purple, and white flowers—pink in the bud—appearing in March and April; 'Rosea', with bronzy leaves and salmon-pink flowers; 'Trailblazer', with dark red young foliage becoming bronzy-green, and white flowers that are pink in the bud.

P. dulcis: The almond, well known as an early spring flowering tree, 7–8 m (23–26 ft) tall, with pink blossom in March. Variety 'Praecox' is earlier, opening in February.

P. × hillieri 'Spire': A 7·5 m (25 ft), conical tree with soft pink flowers and good autumn colours. Often planted as a street tree because of its compact shape.

P. 'Hilling's Weeping': A small weeping tree with an abun-dance of pure white flowers in early April. It will not usually exceed 3 m (10 ft).

P. incisa: The Fuji cherry, a small tree—4–5 m (13–16 ft) tall—covered with pinkish blossom in March, and with good autumn colours.

P. 'Okame': A 4·5 m (15 ft) hybrid cherry that bears clouds of carmine-pink blossom during March.

P. padus: The bird cherry, a 15 m (50 ft) tree native to Britain, with a compact crown and glossy, dark green leaves. The small, fragrant, white flowers grow in drooping racemes during May. There are a few varieties, among them 'Colorata', whose leaves and shoots are purple when young, becoming green in the summer, and which bears pale pink flowers, and 'Watereri', with very large flower clusters.

P. 'Pink Shell': A very beautiful little tree of about 4 m (13 ft), with slender, spreading branches, covered in early April with delicate shell-pink flowers.

P. sargentii: A tree of compact, rounded form, eventually reach-ing 12 m (40 ft). The young leaves are bronze at first, becoming green later, with bright autumn tints. The delicate, pink, single flowers appear in March.

P. serrulata: A wide-spreading, flat-crowned tree seldom

exceeding 4·5 m (15 ft) in height, which bears clusters of double white flowers during April and May. Variety 'Autumn Glory' has pale pink flowers, and fiery autumn foliage colours.

P. subhirtella: A small tree—about 7·5 m (24½ ft)—with pale pink blossom and good autumn colours. There are many fine varieties, including: 'Ascendens Rosea', whose clear shell-pink flowers are tinged with red; 'Autumnalis', the winter-flowering cherry, whose white flowers are produced intermittently from November to March; 'Fukubana', with bright rose-pink flowers borne very abundantly in the spring; and 'Pendula', a slender weeping tree of medium size, bearing very small, pale pink flowers in March and April.

The hybrid Japanese flowering cherries

'Amanogawa': A narrowly columnar tree of great value where planting space is restricted. The semi-double, pale pink flowers appear in April. Maximum height 8 m (26 ft).

'Cheal's Weeping Cherry': A small tree almost identical with 'Kiku-shidare Sakura', and which may be sold under either name. The arching, pendulous branches become laden with double pink flowers during March and April. 2·5 m (8 ft).

'Hisakura': A small tree with coppery young foliage, and single purplish-pink flowers in April. 5 m (16 ft).

'Hokusai': A medium-sized tree with a wide-spreading, vigorous crown, covered in April with large, semi-double pale pink flowers. 6 m (20 ft).

'Jo-nioi': A spreading, vigorous tree with bronzy young leaves, becoming green later, wreathed in fragrant, single white blossom during April. 7 m (23 ft).

'Kanzan': A strong, vigorous, fair-sized tree with upward-slanting branches. One of the most popular varieties, covered during April with dark pink, double blossom. 9 m (30 ft).

'Pink Perfection': A vigorous, medium-sized tree with wide-spreading branches, bearing long, drooping clusters of pale pink double flowers in April and May. 7·5 m (25 ft).

'Shimidsu Sakura': A small tree with a wide-spreading, flattened crown, bearing long, drooping clusters of double flowers that are pink when in the bud, opening white. 5·5 m (17 ft).

'Shirofugen': A medium-sized, vigorous tree with a spreading crown. The leaves are coppery when young, becoming green later. Blossom is pink in the bud, opening white, and lasting very well during April and May. 10 m (33 ft).

'Tai Haku': A very vigorous medium-sized tree whose leaves are coppery-red at first, becoming green as they mature. The

flowers which appear in April are large, single and pure white.
12 m (40 ft).

'Ukon': A vigorous, wide-spreading tree with bronzy young
foliage that becomes green in the summer, only to turn bronze
and red again for the autumn. The blossom is pinkish yellow,
very freely borne during April. 7·5 m (25 ft).

Pseudotsuga menziesii

Douglas fir, a magnificent forest tree for lime-free soils, attaining
60 m (200 ft) in favourable areas. It is propagated by seed. There are
slower-growing varieties, but Douglas fir is not really a suitable
tree for the garden.

Pyrus

The pears. *P. communis* is the garden pear, of which there are many
named varieties, and this makes a valuable shade tree of 10–12 m
(33–40 ft). An old orchard of them forms a splendid basis for a
woodland garden. It is also a beautiful tree in its own right, with its
attractive bark texture, and profuse display of blossom.

P. salicifolia: A very graceful little tree, up to 6 m (20 ft) tall, with
silvery willow-like leaves. The variety 'Pendula' has weeping
branches like a miniature weeping willow, and makes an especially
attractive tree with none of the willow's pushy ways. It grows well
on any soil. The species may be grown from seed, but the variety
should be grafted onto a pear seedling.

Quercus

The oaks, a huge genus of trees both evergreen and deciduous,
natives of many parts of the world. As high-storey trees for planting under, the deciduous oaks are ideal, for their shade is not dense,
and their roots are deep and moderately free from the surface
feeders that disrupt carpeting shrubs. Propagation is from seed.

Q. castaneifolia: The chestnut-leaved oak, a handsome
deciduous tree up to 25 m (83 ft) tall, with leaves not unlike those of
the sweet chestnut. It thrives in any deep, moist soil, and is tolerant
of lime.

Q. cerris: The Turkey oak, a rapidly grown and handsome tree
to 30 m (100 ft), deciduous, thriving in most soils and situations.

Q. coccinea: The scarlet oak, a 23 m (77 ft) deciduous tree with
deeply lobed leaves that turn brilliantly scarlet in the autumn. It
will not do well in limy soils.

Q. frainetto: The Hungarian oak, a magnificent fast-growing
deciduous tree up to 25 m (83 ft), with very long, deeply lobed
leaves. It will grow well in all soil types.

Quercus coccinea (scarlet oak), leaf detail and acorn.

Q. ilex: The holm oak, an impressive evergreen tree which may attain 27 m (90 ft), with leathery, holly-like leaves and roughly fissured bark. It is slow-growing, but thrives in all types of soil.

Q. palustris: The pin oak makes a densely crowned tree of 25 m (83 ft) or more, with branchlets that droop gracefully at their extremities. Deciduous, with deeply lobed leaves that take on fiery autumn colours. It will not grow in limy soils.

Q. petraea: The sessile oak, a native of Britain, by nature chooses the poorer soils of the north and west. A deciduous tree some 25 m (83 ft) tall.

Q. robur: The stalked or English oak prefers the richer, deeper soils of the southern and central parts of England; a similar, deciduous tree also attaining a height of 25 m (83 ft). Few gardeners would want to plant oaks such as these but, where they already exist, very few forest trees are better suited to give shelter to the woodland garden.

Q. rubra: The red oak, a fast-growing, 25 m (83 ft), broad-crowned deciduous tree that takes on good autumn colour. It will not stand a limy soil. The variety 'Aurea' is much smaller, and produces foliage which is yellow in the spring, becoming green later in the season.

Rhamnus imeretinus

This species of buckthorn makes a small tree of around 3 m (10 ft), with handsome, 30 cm (12 in) long leaves of dark green which take on rich purple tints before falling in the autumn. It grows well on all types of soil, particularly in damp, shady sites. Propagation is by seed when this is available, otherwise by means of cuttings taken in the late summer.

Rhus

The sumachs, small deciduous trees often noted for their fiery autumn colours, easily grown, and thriving on any type of soil.

R. chinensis: A broad-crowned tree up to 6 m (20 ft), with terminal panicles of yellowish-white flowers in late summer, and large, coarsely-toothed leaves that colour richly. Propagated by cuttings or air layering.

R. cotinus: The smoke tree, now classified under *Cotinus coggygria.*

R. potaninii: A round-headed tree up to 8 m (26 ft), with long compound leaves and small leaflets. Propagated by cuttings or air layering.

R. typhina: Stag's-horn sumach is a wide-spreading, sparsely branched, 5 m (17 ft) tree, deciduous and displaying bright autumn leaf colours, noted for its thick twigs which are covered with reddish-brown hair, and for the conspicuous, conical fruit clusters that are borne on the ends of the branches. When used as an under-storey shrub, it may be coppiced to the ground every other year. It is propagated from root cuttings taken in December, but suckers can often be removed and transplanted when only a few trees are required.

R. verniciflua: The varnish tree, a handsome, medium sized tree—it may attain 10 m (33 ft) with long, compound leaves and many leaflets. It is used in the East to produce Japanese lacquer. Propagation is by cuttings or air layering.

Robinia

The false acacias are graceful trees with deciduous, finely divided foliage and usually spiny stems and twigs. They are tolerant of all soils and situations, but appreciate it if their crowns are sited in full sunlight. Most of them may be propagated by the suckers which often appear at the roots.

R. × ambigua: A little 3 m (10 ft) tree, with racemes of dainty pink pea-type flowers which appear in June. There is a variety 'Decaisneana' which has a more vigorous habit of growth and larger flowers.

Rhus typhina (stag's horn sumach), noted for its bright autumn leaf colours and for the reddish-brown hair which covers its branches. A conical fruit cluster is shown in this drawing.

R. hispida: The rose acacia, a very small tree, rarely more than 2–3 m (7–10 ft), with showy pink flowers in long racemes, after the manner of a wisteria. It may be grafted onto a stem of common acacia to make a stronger tree.

R. pseudoacacia: The common acacia or robinia makes a picturesque tree approaching 25 m (83 ft) in height. The white, slightly fragrant flowers are produced in long racemes during June. The tree does not take kindly to lopping, and branches which have been shortened almost invariably die back. There is a very attractive, popular variety 'Frisia', which has rich yellow leaves throughout the summer.

Salix

The willows are incomparable for the waterside and on heavy, moist ground, but they will thrive in other soils and situations, too. All are deciduous, and all strike very readily from cuttings. Often, however, the most convenient way of propagating tree willows is to plant 'sets' or 'truncheons'. These are whole branches of a convenient size and shape, removed after the leaves fall in the autumn. In the case of a weeping willow, for instance, a set may be up to 3 m (10 ft) long and 2–3 cm ($\frac{3}{4}$–1$\frac{1}{2}$ in) wide. About 45 cm (18 in), or up to a third of the length, is planted firmly in peaty ground, and a stake is inserted. Sets are often placed directly into their permanent sites.

S. alba: The white willow, a familiar tree of the river bank and marshy places, and a parent of many hybrids. It will attain 24 m (80 ft).

S. babylonica: The weeping willow of Babylon. This handsome 15 m (50 ft) tree was planted in gardens for many years, but has now largely been superseded by the golden weeping willow S. × *chrysocoma*.

S. caprea: The goat willow, a 7 m (23 ft) British tree that grows widely in damp places, and produces 'pussy willow' and 'palm'.

S. 'Chermesina': A variety with brilliantly scarlet bark on the younger branches, and also known as 'Britzensis'. It is often grown as a coppicing shrub to provide colour during the winter months, in which case the stems must be cut hard back to the base, every other year in early spring. To form a pollarded tree for its winter colour, 'Chermesina' should be allowed to form a stem of the desired height, and the cutting back is then done to the point where the crown is required to branch. If allowed to grow into a full-sized tree it may attain 24 m (80 ft).

S. × chrysocoma: The golden weeping willow, one of the most popular of garden trees for its beauty at all seasons, its hardiness and vigour. It really needs a great deal of room as it makes a large tree, attaining 18 m (60 ft) or more, but it can be grown where space is limited, provided the most vigorous branches are removed.

S. cinerea: The grey sallow, a tough little 3 m (10 ft) British tree that has often been used successfully in the reclamation of slag heaps and waste ground.

S. fragilis: The crack willow, a large and familiar, wide-ranging tree that grows with the white willow along river and stream banks. Eventually it will attain 27 m (90 ft).

S. viminalis: The osier, a small willow reaching 6 m (20 ft), with numerous named varieties cultivated for basket making.

S. 'Vitellina': Of similar size and habit to 'Chermesina' and requiring identical treatment when grown for its showy winter-coloured bark, which in this case is a bright orange-yellow.

Sequoia sempervirens

The California redwood is an attractive tree with its spongy, reddish-brown bark and dark, yew-like evergreen leaves. It tends to outgrow the average garden, however, and in California it has held the record as the world's tallest tree, around 110 m (367 ft), though there are other contenders for the title. Normally grown from seed, it will take from cuttings placed in a closed frame, and is unusual among conifers in producing coppice growth from felled stumps. It will succeed in any type of soil.

Sequoiadendron giganteum

Wellingtonia, the 'Big Tree' of California—it beats the redwood in girth, but comes second in height. These trees are said to live for over three thousand years. Propagation is by seed, and they are reasonably lime-tolerant. They make very beautiful avenue and park trees, and are remarkable for their very thick, spongy bark.

Sorbus

The whitebeams and rowans. A group of ornamental trees with attractive foliage, usually white flowers in the spring, and showy berries in the autumn. All are deciduous, and will grow on all types of soil. Propagation is by seed in the case of the true species, and this should be sown as soon as it is ripe, but the named varieties should be budded or grafted onto seedling stocks.

S. aria: The common whitebeam, a 10 m (33 ft) tree often seen growing wild on limestone soils in the south of England, but it is hardy farther north and is useful as a shelter tree by the sea, or in grimy industrial areas. The leaves are green on the upper surfaces, felted white below, and colour well in the autumn, when the berries are a deep crimson. Varieties include: 'Chrysophylla', whose leaves are yellow throughout the summer; 'Decaisneana', with larger leaves and berries; 'Lutescens', with downy, grey leaves; and 'Pendula', a graceful, weeping form with slender, willow-like leaves.

S. aucuparia: The mountain ash or rowan, a familiar British tree attaining 15 m (50 ft), noted for its abundance of usually bright red berries. Very widely planted, it thrives on most types of soil and is especially tolerant of poor, acid sites. Garden varieties include: 'Aspleniifolia', with finely-cut, fern-like leaves; 'Beissneri', with coppery coloured bark and dark red young shoots supporting deeply-cut, yellowish leaves; 'Shearwater Seedling', a vigorous, upright variety with heavy bunches of orange-red berries; and 'Xanthocarpa', with yellow berries that last on the tree longer than the red type.

S. domestica: The service tree, a medium-sized—up to 15 m (50 ft)—species that is sometimes cultivated for its edible, apple-like fruits.

S. 'Embley': A 7·5 m (25 ft) erect-growing rowan bearing huge bunches of glossy, orange berries. Colours well in autumn.

Sorbus aucuparia (mountain ash or rowan), noted for its abundance of red berries.

S. hupehensis: A vigorous, erect-growing 10 m (33 ft) tree with purplish branches and blue-green foliage that colours brightly in the autumn. The berries are white, in drooping clusters, and last well on the tree.

S. 'Gibbsii': A small, compact hybrid tree with whitebeam-like leaves and conspicuously large red berries in huge clusters. It will attain a height of 7 m (23 ft).

S. 'Joseph Rock': An outstanding rowan of some 8 m (26 ft), with rich autumn foliage colour, and creamy-yellow berries.

S. sargentiana: A highly acclaimed medium-sized rowan, about 7·5 m (24 ft) tall, with red-stalked leaves, huge bunches of small but showy scarlet berries, and large red sticky winter buds.

S. torminalis: The wild service tree, a 23 m (77 ft) native of Britain, picturesquely proportioned with a rough, scaly bark, maple-like leaves and speckled brown berries sometimes called 'chequers'. The foliage colours well in the autumn.

S. vilmorinii: A graceful little tree, seldom exceeding 5 m (17 ft) with a spreading crown and dainty, fern-like foliage which turns richly purple and crimson in the autumn. The pale pink berries in drooping clusters are especially attractive.

Stewartia pseudocamellia

An unusual little deciduous tree which loves a moist woodland site that is free from lime. In the right surroundings, it may exceed a height of 10 m (33 ft). The bark is picturesque and peeling in flakes, and camellia-like white flowers are produced in succession during July and August. The leaves colour well in the autumn before they are shed. Propagation is by 7–10 cm (3–4 in) side-shoot cuttings taken early in June and set in a closed, shaded frame.

Stranvaesia davidiana

An evergreen tree of 7–8 m (23–26 ft), though it may be grown as a large shrub—resembling a cotoneaster with its erect branches and leathery, dark green leaves. It bears clusters of white flowers in June, followed by drooping bunches of brilliant crimson berries which persist over winter. It grows well in sun or shade, in any soil or situation. Propagation is by seed, but in the case of varieties, such as the yellow-berried 'Fructuluteo' which may not come true from seed, strong shoots of the current season's growth may be layered: a slight twist should be made 15 cm (6 in) from the tip, and the shoot should be pegged down firmly.

Styrax japonica

A beautiful little evergreen tree up to 5 m (17 ft) tall, sometimes grown as a large shrub, which succeeds in moist, shady situations that are free from lime. The variety 'Fargesii' is more tree-like in habit. The gracefully spreading, fan-like branches are hung with white bell-shaped flowers in June—the main reason why this plant should be grown as a tree rather than a shrub, enabling the flowers to be admired from below. It may be propagated from seed if any is produced, otherwise shoots may be layered in a peaty compost, or side-shoot cuttings with a heel may be taken in June or July.

Syringa

The lilacs are hardy small trees—they will rarely exceed 6 m (20 ft)—or large shrubs which flourish in any soil or situation, though they need some sun to do their best. The gloriously fragrant flowers appear in May and June. All are deciduous. Propagation is by means of layering in the spring—it is usually more convenient to practise air layering. There are so many lovely varieties to choose from, both single and double-flowered, that choice is difficult, especially as many of the varieties are almost identical. Some of the best and most distinct are:

'Belle de Nancy' Double, lilac-pink, purple-red when in bud;
'Capitaine Baltet' Single, carmine-pink;

'Charles Joly' Double, dark purple-red;
'Congo' Single, deep lilac-red;
'Edith Cavell' Double, pure white, creamy-yellow when in bud;
'Etna' Single, deep claret-purple;
'Jan van Tol' Single, pure white;
'Katherine Havemeyer' Double, lavender-pink;
'Madame Abel Chatenay' Double, bluish-white;
'Madame Antoine Buchner' Double, rose-pink;
'Madame Lemoine' Double, pure white;
'Marceau' Single, claret-purple;
'Marechal Foch' Single, bright carmine-rose;
'Mrs Edward Harding' Double, claret-red;
'President Grevy' Double, lilac-blue;
'Souvenir d'Alice Harding' Double, pure white;
'Souvenir de Louis Spaeth' Single, wine-red.

Taxodium distichum

The swamp cypress, a deciduous conifer of unusual beauty, with fibrous reddish-brown bark and bright, ferny foliage which takes on autumn colours before falling. It is the best conifer for growing in waterlogged places, where it will attain over 30 m (100 ft) and develop huge buttresses and protuberant roots. If it is used for planting in wet places, however, it is important to build a dry mound of soil to receive the young plant; once the roots are firmly established, it will thrive where few other trees will grow, but it is not suitable for limy soils. Propagation is by seed.

Thuja

Hardy evergreen conifers very like *Chamaecyparis*, but they have slightly broader leaf sprays which, when crushed, have a pleasant, orangey smell; crushed *Chamaecyparis* leaves smell turpentiney and rather unpleasant. Propagation is by seed, or 7–8 cm (3 in) cuttings taken in September and set in a closed frame. Varieties may also be grafted.

T. occidentalis: The American arborvitae, a hardy, graceful 18 m (60 ft) tree with wide-spreading, upcurved branches which form a broadly columnar crown. There are numerous garden varieties, including several rock garden dwarfs such as the popular 'Rheingold'.

T. plicata: Western red cedar, a fast-growing 40 m (130 ft) ornamental tree which is also frequently planted as a forest timber tree. There are numerous garden varieties, among them 'Zebrina', a very beautiful gold-variegated tree of excellent shape and vigour, of a colour which stands out well in the woodland garden. It will stand clipping as a hedge and may be grown as a trimmed shrub.

Tilia

The limes, a group of large, deciduous trees which thrive in all types of soil and situation. They are very tolerant of pruning, and are often 'pleached' to form archways and other garden features. They may be propagated by seed when this is available, otherwise by air layering.

T. cordata: The small-leaved lime which grows wild in Britain, a 23 m (75 ft) tree with heart-shaped leaves 5–6 cm (2 in) long, and wide clusters of small, fragrant, yellowish-white flowers in July.

T. × euchlora: A graceful tree with a somewhat weeping habit, attaining about 25 m (85 ft) in height. It makes a useful replacement for elms which have died from Dutch elm disease.

T. × europaea: The common lime, a vigorous tree up to 30 m (100 ft) or more, frequently planted in the past as a roadside and avenue tree, and usually with a dense growth of young shoots around the bole.

T. petiolaris: The weeping lime, a very beautiful and majestic 20 m (67 ft) tree, with gracefully weeping branches.

T. platyphyllos: The broad-leaved lime, another large tree which may reach 30 m (100 ft), it has broad, sharply-toothed leaves which are downy on the undersurface. There are several varieties, the best of which is 'Rubra', the red-twigged lime, probably the most commonly planted lime when commemorative or street trees are needed.

Tsuga

The hemlocks are elegant evergreen conifers with very dainty foliage. The species are propagated from seed, but the garden varieties may be grown from shoot cuttings 7–8 cm (3 in) long, taken in July and struck in a shaded frame. As with some other conifers such as the spruces, it is desirable to take cuttings from the leading tips of branches if the variety is of an upright-growing form, otherwise subsequent growth will be bushy and branch-like. For weeping or spreading varieties, however, lateral shoots are just as satisfactory.

T. canadensis: The eastern hemlock makes a forked, broadly spreading tree from which the lower limbs tend to crotch themselves into the ground and from there form separate, ascending trunks. It bears shade fairly well and is tolerant of limy soils, but because of its spreading habit eventually takes up a great deal of room. There are many dwarf varieties, but the species will exceed 10 m (33 ft).

T. heterophylla: The western hemlock is a well-shaped, fast-growing, 18 m (60 ft) tree with a graceful, spire-like crown. When

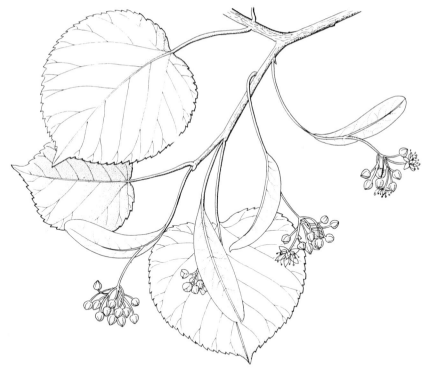

Tilia platyphyllos (broad-leaved lime). The well-known red-twigged lime is a variety of this tree.

young, it grows well in shade and has often been used to under-plant other trees—it will take far more readily in such a woodland situation, than when planted on a bare, open site. It is not tolerant of limy soils, but otherwise western hemlock is one of the most useful conifers for the woodland garden.

Ulmus

The many species and varieties of elm have not been planted to any great extent since Dutch elm disease took such a heavy toll. There are many stately trees which can profitably be used instead.

3
Tree Care

'Thinning' in the forestry sense may occasionally become necessary in the woodland garden when over-storey trees are beginning to suppress their neighbours irreparably but, ninety-nine times out of a hundred, the thinning we do will be limited to the removal of individual branches rather than whole stems.

The art of shaping any tree crown consists in increasing the intensity of light reaching the under-storey plants, while at the same time retaining, or enhancing, the full natural beauty of the tree. Every tree species—and in many cases each variety within the species—possesses its own unique habit of growth. It is this very characteristic that gives the woodland garden special charm. When a stem is lopped or branches shortened without regard to form, a valuable effect may be lost.

Street trees in many cases are heavily lopped, and such work is not necessarily out of place. The planes of London and other cities are kept healthily in bounds by means of judicious pruning, and the results are perfect for their environment. Such a method would not be acceptable within the woodland garden context, except in those cases where a specialized effect is required—willows, for example, may be pollarded to produce colourful young shoots. This technique is described in Chapter 8.

Certainly, some clearing work will sooner or later become necessary to counter the continuing process of natural woodland succession that would lead eventually to almost pure stands of the tallest-growing, most light excluding species. But we are not in the business of growing timber, neither, as a rule, are we using timber-producing species. The recurrent theme around which we must build our variations is a judicial removal of the whole branch flush with the trunk. A shortened branch, more often than not, will have lost much of its natural elegance for ever, and such curtailment should be carried out only where a convenient sub-lateral branch is in a position to camouflage the amputation.

Thinning the crown.

Raising the crown

Removing the lowest limbs of the crown can often be done without in the least upsetting the balance of the tree as a whole, and as these lowest branches are normally the ones which carry the greatest weight of leaves—and therefore those which cast the most shade—the amount of light that can be admitted by even the most cautious of operations is quite remarkable. Most light reaching the ground, after all, does so from all sides rather than from directly overhead.

Such pruning can usually be done in the summer, when the intensity of shade and the possible effects of admitting light can better be judged. When carried out at this season it usually avoids, too, the production of vigorous new shoots that often follows heavy winter pruning. Care, however, should be taken with trees that tend to bleed a lot, such as the birch—which, anyway, is so lightly branched that live pruning is seldom needed—or the horse chestnut and some conifers, which are better left until November.

Incidentally, too heavy a summer pruning can sometimes result in a 'shock' effect caused by the sudden change brought about in the tree's metabolism. I have seen otherwise healthy oaks have their leaves turn yellow within days, following a heavy summer pruning. A reasonably reliable rule is to shape the crowns of quick-growing ornamental hardwoods in the summer, but to leave work on conifers and the slow-growing, large forest trees until the growing season has finished.

Thinning the crown

This operation entails the complete removal of branches from within the crown proper. Very careful thought should be given to the choice of branches to be removed; if there are several angles of vision, it is a good idea to stand well back and study the tree from all sides, trying to imagine what the results of the work will be before a start is made. One should always look at those main branches that need to be retained, and the outline of their foliage, trying to blank out in the mind's eye those parts of the crown to be removed.

The effects of crown thinning correctly carried out are immediate and twofold: the amount of light penetrating the canopy may be doubled at least; and the appearance of the tree is often improved beyond recognition. The cedar of Lebanon is a somewhat untidy tree by nature. A mature specimen, untouched, will be congested in the crown, full of dead branches and a mass of suppressed twigs. But in famous gardens throughout the temperate regions of the world, we see cedars whose noble limbs are perfect in symmetry, clean, uncluttered and healthy. They clearly demonstrate the value of such treatment.

Most people when pruning err on the side of excessive caution, and this is a good fault, because, obviously, a branch once removed cannot be replaced. But the idea behind crown thinning is not merely to remove dead and dying wood and those branches which are completely suppressed; the operation must significantly increase the amount of light penetrating the foliage. Dead wood in any case should be removed as a matter of course—but in any tree there are branches which are destined to become suppressed in time. Nature's own way of pruning is slow, and not always what we want to see in our gardens; what we are doing in practising crown shaping is to anticipate nature—to remove those branches which probably would in any case have died, long before the tree's peak of maturity is reached.

Not all trees have one central stem, of course. Many have a framework of large limbs, which must each be treated during this operation as though they were a main trunk, and all branches to be removed must be cut flush to them. For the small under-storey tree, crown thinning is no less beneficial. The rule to follow when working with under-storey plants is: if a plant has the makings of a small tree, then encourage the formation of a distinct trunk and symmetrical crown. If, on the other hand, a plant is plainly a shrub by nature, then make sure it retains the contours of a shrub, and does not aspire to adopt an uncharacteristic shape.

Needless to say, shaping the crowns of large trees is highly skilled and hazardous work. But, apart from the obvious danger to one's own life and limb, it is all too easy to damage the tree by tearing the trunk or skinning the bark. 'Cowboy' tree surgeons can spoil a beautiful tree irreparably, so the garden owner should make sure that anybody employed to this end knows exactly what he is doing, and also that both parties have the same end result in mind, for ideas on what is fitting can be widely at variance.

Another important point that is often overlooked until too late, is never to burn or allow branches to be burned under or near the canopy of growing trees. The concentration of heat immediately above a fire and to the leeward of it is intense, and can kill foliage or branches.

Pruning technique

Any pruning scar on the trunk should be almost flush with the surrounding bark, bearing in mind that, unless the wound is too large, the bark in healing will grow over the scar. It follows that:

a) the stump must not be too prominent for this healing process to take place, otherwise the stump itself will be sure to die back;
b) in the case of large branches the cut should not be *too* flush, otherwise the area to be healed will be much larger than necessary;
c) the exposed wood must be protected from attack by fungal disease during the healing process. In the case of very large pruning scars that cannot possibly heal over, permanent protection is necessary; every scar on a main stem should be treated with Arbrex or some other bituminous tree paint. Stockholm tar is a useful alternative.

When cutting branches thus close to the stem, there is always the probability that the weight of the severed branch as it sags will tear a portion of bark and cambium away from the main stem. Small branches should always be supported in one hand while sawing with the other. In the case of larger branches, these should invariably be shortened to a stump before making the final cut, and in this case it is the stump that has to be supported to avoid damage. The shortening cut should be in two stages, the first of which is an undercut to the point where the saw starts to jam. On very long branches, it may be necessary to shorten them more than once in this way.

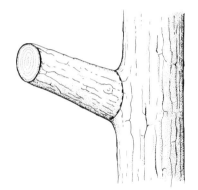

It is advisable to cut off a large branch in two stages: first shorten it to a stump and then cut off the stump so that it is flush with the main stem, supporting it with one hand as you do so.

Very large limbs among the crown must be lowered gently with ropes, not only to avoid the dangers already outlined, but also because the butt of a falling limb, springing back unchecked, can seriously damage the bark at the base of the tree.

While heavy lopping may be a professional's job, pruning branches of more manageable size is not usually considered so. A ladder is often needed to reach the branch, and one of the commonest ladder accidents is liable to happen during this shortening of a long branch prior to the final cut. It is almost like the old joke about sawing through the branch you are sitting on—but it is a real danger that is often not apparent until too late. When a branch is shortened drastically, its weight is reduced equally drastically, especially when in full leaf. Such a branch will spring up perhaps by an arm's length or more as the weight is relieved, and the ladder which was leaning against it so securely a moment before is suddenly supported by nothing at all.

Cavity repair

Decay in the stem usually results from the depredations of a fungus attacking the tree. It may have entered via the roots or through the bark, or it may have originated when an incorrectly pruned limb has resulted in a dead stump. The fungus causing decay may be parasitic—attacking living plant tissue—or it may be saprophytic—feeding on material that is already dead. However, once commenced, cavity decay is unlikely to check itself unaided, especially where the situation is such as to allow rain water to enter and saturate the wood.

In the case of slow-growing, heavy timbered trees such as oak or yew, butt rot or basal decay is common, from any of a variety of causes, but the spread of infection upwards and outwards may be so gradual that little harm, from an amenity point of view, is done.

With the lighter, softer wood of such species as horse chestnut, European sycamore, and many small ornamental trees, the spread of decay can be very rapid indeed. The important thing in avoiding trouble from cavities, of course, is not to allow them to happen; but when they have already appeared and the damage is done, treatment should be undertaken without delay.

Basically there are two lines of approach, both of which have their professional adherents: the open cavity, and the filled cavity. By and large, the alternative we choose will be prompted by practical considerations, but in either case the decayed wood must be removed very thoroughly so that the interior of the cavity is cut back smoothly into clean, fungus-free timber—and this is much easier to say than to do. Once the wound is clean, it should be washed with a fungicide such as Cuprinol to kill any fungus spores remaining.

In the case of a small cavity with a large entrance, no insuperable difficulty should present itself—but in the great majority of cases, the situation is reversed; the cavity is large or of unknown extent, and the entry hole is small and difficult of access.

Frequently, the job entails cutting out perhaps sound timber and enlarging the hole. A small chain saw is the most useful tool for this job, but it can rarely be used to effect actually inside the cavity—though there are extensible chipper attachments available for professional use. In practice, circumstances vary so widely—and no one case is quite like any other—that cavity clearing becomes largely a matter of ingenuity, with a strong element of trial and error.

If the treated cavity is to be left open, the important thing is to ensure that water is not going to stand inside. It is common practice to drill a hole from the outside, slanting slightly upwards into the base of the cavity, and to fit a piece of pipe so that any water can drain away before it has the chance to initiate further decay. When this is done, and when circumstances permit, professional tree surgeons often fix a wire mesh over the entrance to prevent birds nesting in the hole and clogging up the pipe with their nesting material.

Many environmentally conscious people would consider this to be a case of inverted priorities, of course. Hole-nesting birds are so dependent on finding suitable nesting sites, and such a specialized requirement as this must be a powerful factor influencing the distribution of desirable woodland birds such as the woodpeckers, owls, and the many small tree-dwelling species—and larger birds too—that rely on these sites. But even though our concern for the environmental problems of wild creatures prompts us to leave tree cavities unsealed, this is not the same as leaving them untreated. All exposed accessible surfaces should be painted with bituminous paint or Arbrex, whatever method is adopted.

Arbrex may also be used as a mastic to bind together sawdust and sand when it is decided to fill very small cavities, after cleaning, but as this mixture never becomes really firm, it is apt to wash out of the hole if rain can reach it. Concrete has often been used in the past for filling large cavities, especially those at or near ground level, where there is not likely to be much swaying movement of the tree, which would cause it to crack. A much more reliable filler, and more convenient to handle, is the cold bituminous tarmac available in plastic bags and intended for repairs to drives.

Another method of filling is based on liquid urethane foam, which is applied in the form of two liquids. They are poured together into the cavity, and the resultant chemical activity produces an expanding foam that completely fills every unseen crevice. This foam hardens within minutes, and any excess filler protruding through the hole is then trimmed off and a sealing coat of Arbrex applied. The filling must not be allowed to protrude beyond the cambium so that, provided the area is not too large, the bark will grow over the repair and, in time, completely cover it. Various other compounds have been used besides those mentioned, and experiments are constantly being undertaken by interested professional bodies.

4

The Under-Storey

It is evident that our woodland community can consist, firstly, of fairly tall, light-demanding trees that themselves cast very little shade. Below these there may be a secondary crown level formed by species which require less light. The under-storey proper which occupies the next stratum will consist of shrubs which prefer a comparatively low intensity of light. The ground beneath these will now be quite overshadowed; only a few specialized plants will survive, and weeds should find themselves excluded. But wherever there is sufficient light around and between the shrubs, the ground-hugging layer of woodland herbs and creeping shrubs will thrive in company with ferns and bulbs.

Our choice of under-storey plants cannot be made entirely by rule of thumb; everything depends on the locality, the site, and the individual planting spot available. Optimum height of the plant is of paramount importance; whether it will stand much shade or little; whether it enjoys an acid or a limy soil—they are all factors which have to be taken into account.

The selection of under-storey plants which follows is graduated more or less by height—the average height they may be expected to have reached by the time they are comfortably mature; it would be misleading to attempt to be more accurate than this.

Propagation

The note on the technique of air-layering included in Chapter 2 applies equally to small trees and large shrubs. By and large, cuttings taken from shrubs root more readily than those taken from trees. As it is usually the smaller under-storey plants that need massing, and therefore propagating most frequently, notes on the technique best suited to each have been given in some detail. If all else fails, shoots will often produce roots if they are stood in a jar of water and left over winter on the window sill, to be potted up and planted out in the spring or in the following autumn.

Taxus baccata

HT

3 ft)

The common yew; with Scots pine and juniper, one of the only three conifers that are native to Britain. An under-storey tree, tolerant of all types of soil and unpromising situations, and itself casting heavy shade. The almost black appearance of the foliage makes it a valuable background plant, and there is a full-sized variety, 'Lutea', whose yellow berries stand out more vividly in contrast than the usual red kind. The columnar and prostrate forms are of great garden value, and these are included in their appropriate height category. The typical species will grow readily from seed, but the varieties must be propagated by cuttings of terminal shoots, 5–8 cm (2–3 in) long, taken in July and placed in a shaded frame.

Prunus laurocerasus

(22 ft)

The laurel makes a very dense, vigorous, evergreen background screen and under-storey shrub, but does not grow well on shallow chalk soils. The white flowers in April are very attractive. Propagated from side-shoots taken with a heel during September, and placed in sandy beds outdoors.

Embothrium coccineum

The Chilean firebush, a wonderful semi-evergreen shrub or small tree producing masses of orange-scarlet flowers during May and June. It needs a sheltered woodland clearing with side-shade, and a deep, moist soil that is free from lime. It is normally grown from seed, but root cuttings may be taken in December. These are cut into 5 cm (2 in) lengths and potted singly in a sandy compost.

Ilex aquifolium

Holly, one of the most useful hardy evergreen woodland plants for all soil types, whether grown as a small tree or a bush. There are numerous varieties: 'Golden Queen' and 'Silver Queen' are attractive, but do not bear berries; 'Golden King' has a bright yellow leaf margin and also bears berries; *I. latifolia* has immense dark green leaves and orange-red berries. Hollies may be layered in the autumn, or cuttings of side-shoots with a heel may be taken during the summer: the bark on one side of the shoots should be scraped before setting them in a sandy compost, directly into pots placed under a shaded frame.

Buxus sempervirens

20 ft)

Box—the compactness of this evergreen shrub or small tree, with its dense mass of tiny dark leaves, and its ability to thrive in all types

HEIGHT

6 m (20 ft)

of soil make it especially useful for screening work. There are numerous dwarf-growing varieties, and all these may be raised from 10 cm (4 in) cuttings of side-shoots or tips, taken in September and set in open beds.

Eucryphia × intermedia 'Rostrevor' and Eucryphia × nymansensis 'Nymansay'

Evergreen small trees or large shrubs of rapid growth, requiring a sheltered position with side-shade and a lime-free soil. They become wreathed with showy, fragrant white flowers during August and September. They may be grown from seed if this is available, otherwise from 7 cm (3 in) cuttings of side-shoots taken with a heel. Layering during the summer is also effective: a twist is made about 15 cm (6 in) from the tip of a suitable strong shoot, and this is pegged down firmly.

Prunus lusitanica

5·5 m (18 ft)

Portuguese laurel is really attractive when allowed to grow into a tree with a clean stem, as even quite young plants develop a characteristically gnarled appearance. It can also be used as a branching shrub, and on shallow chalk soils it may be used in preference to common laurel, as it thrives on all sites. It has glossy, dark, evergreen, red-stemmed leaves and attractive racemes of white flower in April. There is a variegated cultivar 'Variegata'. Propagation is achieved by means of side-shoot cuttings taken with a heel during summer and set in a frame, or similar but harder cuttings taken in November and set in open, sandy beds.

Taxus baccata 'Elegantissima'

The golden yew, a densely foliaged form with ascending branches, of very good colour, but at its best when positioned where the sun's rays can strike the leaves. It may be propagated by terminal shoot cuttings, 5–8 cm (2–3 in) long, taken in July and set in a shaded frame.

Hamamelis mollis

5 m (17 ft)

The witch hazel, a deciduous tree or many-branched tall shrub, noted for the unusual, sweetly scented flowers that appear on the bare twigs from December to March, remaining unscathed during the coldest of winters. It thrives in any soil type. Good varieties include: 'Aurantiaca', an upright small tree with thick clusters of orange-yellow flowers; 'Coombe Wood', a spreading form with large yellow strongly-scented flowers; 'Goldcrest', with richly golden-yellow flowers flushed with red; and 'Pallida', with large

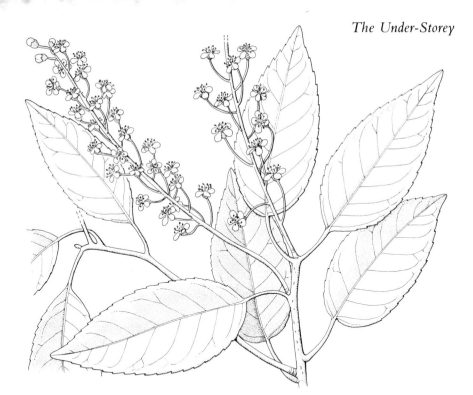

Prunus lusitanica (Portuguese laurel) has attractive racemes of white flowers in April.

(17 ft) sulphur-yellow flowers. Both species and varieties may be propagated by layering strong shoots in the early spring, making a cut about 25 cm (10 in) from the tip and setting fairly deeply in a sandy loam, pegging down firmly. Air layering is usually a more convenient method.

Elaeagnus pungens

A very vigorous, spreading evergreen, the leaves shiny green on the upper surfaces and silver beneath. The best variety is 'Maculata' with bright, gold-splashed leaves, a most handsome shrub when viewed against the darker greens of yew and Portuguese laurel. The variety 'Aureo-variegata' appears to be the same. It grows well on all types of soil except shallow chalk. Propagation is by cuttings of side-shoots up to 10 cm (4 in) long, taken either at a node or with a slight heel, preferably during July, and set in a shaded frame. Alternatively, shoots may be layered in September, first making a twist in the stem about 30 cm (12 in) from the tip, and pegging into sandy soil.

Elaeagnus × ebbingei

For any soil or situation, in woodland or as a wind-resistant shelter by the sea, this fast-growing evergreen is hard to beat. Its large

n (15 ft)

4·5 m (15 ft)

leaves are green above and silver beneath, it bears fragrant flowers in the autumn and orange fruits in the spring. Propagation is the same as for *E. pungens*.

Corylus maxima

The filbert nut is like a larger version of the hazel, and often cultivated for its nuts. Variety 'Purpurea' has beautiful purple leaves, and is worthy of a place in any woodland garden. It prefers a neutral or acid soil, but will grow on limy types provided they have a good depth. Like the hazel, it is deciduous. Propagation is by layering in the autumn; a strong shoot should be twisted about 30 cm (12 in) from the tip and pegged down.

Rhododendron

4 m (13 ft)

The taller species and varieties. There are hundreds of rhododendrons and azaleas, which are included in the same genus. The dwarfer-growing forms are often best in full sun, but most are by nature woodland plants, and the choice open for woodland gardening is immense. All need a lime-free soil, and may be propagated by layering: strong shoots—twisted slightly and pegged down after growth has finished in late summer—are slow to root but fairly sure. The best species include: *R. augustinii*, blue flowered and fast growing, it has a variety 'Electra' with deep violet-blue flowers in April and May; *R. mucronulatum* is the remarkable winter-flowering rhododendron, medium sized and often deciduous, with a welcome show of rosy-purple during January and February; *R. barbatum* has attractive peeling bark and glowing crimson flowers in March; *R. thomsonii*, seen at its best at Bodnant, where the vivid ruby flowers contrast unforgettably with the dark green cypresses behind; *R. nuttallii* has huge, fragrant, light yellow flowers and *R. lacteum* has smaller but perfectly shaped yellow flowers; *R. souliei* makes a beautifully shaped bush with symmetrical foliage, the flowers varying in shades from white through pink to crimson when the buds are opening. Some of the best named varieties are: 'Alice', with pink flowers in May; 'Angelo', fragrant white, May; 'Argosy', white with crimson at the base of each petal and fragrant, June; 'Auriel', pink, June; 'Aurora', pink, April; 'Avalanche', white with red at the base, April; 'Beauty of Littleworth', white, spotted with crimson, May; 'Bibiani', crimson, May; 'Biskra', vermilion, April; 'Calrose', pink, May; 'Chanticleer', crimson-scarlet, May; 'China', creamy white, May; 'Cornubia', crimson, March; 'Countess of Derby', pink, May; 'Cynthia', crimson, May; 'Dame Nellie Melba', pink, spotted with crimson, May; 'Dusky Maid', dark red,

3·7 m (12 ft)

June; 'Fire-bird', salmon-red, May; 'Fulgarb', crimson, February;

Rhododendron augustinii. This handsome species has blue flowers and is fast growing.

■ (12 ft) 'Grenadier', blood-red, June; 'Jacquetta', red, May; 'Ladybird', pink, May; 'Lady Digby', blood-red, May; 'Loderi', several varieties ranging from creamy white to pink, and all very fragrant, April; 'Moser's Maroon', maroon-red, June; 'Mount Everest', white, April; 'Mrs A. M. Williams', crimson-scarlet, May; 'Mrs J. C. Williams', white marked with crimson, June; 'Pink Glory', pink, April; 'Russellianum', lavender-blue, May; 'Shilsonii', blood-red, April; 'Susan', mauve, May; 'Wonderland', yellowish white, June.

Elaeagnus macrophylla

A very handsome, spreading, evergreen shrub for shelter or screen, it does well on most sites but does not like a shallow soil over chalk. The rounded leaves are silvery on both surfaces in the spring, becoming green above later in the season. The flowers in autumn are inconspicuous but fragrant, and red fruits appear in the spring. Propagation is effected by layering in September, making a twist about 30 cm (12 in) from the tip of a strong shoot before pegging it down. Air layering is usually more convenient, or alternatively ■ (12 ft) side-shoot cuttings may be taken in July and set in a shaded frame.

Taxus baccata 'Fastigiata'

HEIGHT

3·5 m (12 ft)

The Irish yew, a familiar, upright tree often planted in church-yards, forming a dense column of tightly packed, very dark green branches. The upright variety 'Fastigiata Aureomarginata', is the golden Irish yew—a very handsome form but, like all golden varieties, it needs the sun for its colour to be retained well. Irish yew is useful as a backing for low, spreading shrubs, but it should not be overshaded too heavily, or its symmetry will be lost. Propagation is achieved by taking the stout terminal shoots, about 10 cm (4 in) long, and setting them in a shaded frame during July.

Eucryphia glutinosa

A deciduous shrub or small tree that needs a sheltered woodland site that is free from lime. It becomes well covered with showy white flowers during July and August, and the foliage colours well in the autumn before the leaves are shed. It may be propagated by seed, or by cuttings of heeled side-shoots taken in June or July and set directly into small pots under a shaded frame. Layering is also a successful method.

Phillyrea decora

3·2 m (11 ft)

A handsome, evergreen, densely rounded bush with large leathery leaves, small fragrant white flowers in the spring, and purple-black plum-like fruits. It succeeds in all types of soil and situation. For propagation, side-shoot cuttings about 10 cm (4 in) long, with a heel, are taken in August. Alternatively, layering may be carried out in the autumn, in which case a tongue should be cut about 35 cm (14 in) from the tip of a strong shoot, which is then pegged down into a sandy soil.

Mahonia 'Charity'

A splendid evergreen shrub with spiny, almost holly-like leaves. The magnificent deep yellow flowers are borne aloft in long racemes during autumn and early winter. The mahonias are valued for their tolerance of all soil conditions. Air layering is usually the most successful method of propagation.

Mahonia japonica

A similar evergreen shrub to 'Charity', thriving equally well in poor soils which may be quite strongly alkaline. It has showy, drooping racemes of lemon-yellow flowers produced in the autumn and lasting through winter. Propagation is best achieved by air layering in the spring. Roots will usually have appeared by

3 m (10 ft)

the autumn and the young plant should be potted up for the winter.

76

Mahonia 'Charity'. Evergreen shrub with holly-like leaves and deep yellow flowers.

Fatsia japonica

(10 ft) A wonderfully architectural plant, with large, shiny, dark green leaves, this spreading evergreen has an exotic appearance. White globular flowers appear in clusters at the ends of the branches in October. It grows well in all types of soil, and does well at the seaside. Propagation is by 10–12 cm (4–5 in) cuttings taken in August.

Corylus avellana

Hazel, the nut tree found in British woodlands and which thrives in any soil. It may be trained as a small tree, but is usually seen as a many-stemmed shrub. Hazel is deciduous, but it is very attractive during February when the catkins appear. The variety 'Aurea' is a very pleasant yellow-leaved form, and 'Contorta' has curiously twisted stems. Propagation may be achieved by layering in the autumn, when shoots should be pegged down after being twisted about 30 cm (12 in) from the tip. The variety 'Contorta' is difficult to layer satisfactorily and is usually budded or grafted onto normal
(9 ft) plants.

Fatsia japonica, a spreading evergreen of exotic appearance. Note the globular flowers which appear at the ends of branches.

Juniperus × media 'Pfitzerana'

2·7 m (9 ft) The wide-spreading branches of this conifer are useful for softening hard outlines and covering eye-sores. Easily grown in any soil type, it does well in shade, retaining its typical shape even in completely sunless situations. Attractive variegated forms are available, and there is a handsome gold-tipped variety, 'Aurea', but these need some sun to retain their colour. All the varieties grow from cuttings taken in late summer, and large plants may be obtained by layering: a suitable branch near ground level should be partially severed near the stem, and the leaves removed from the part that is to be rooted below the surface. It is not necessary to peg the shoot upright.

Aucuba japonica

A very handsome, hardy evergreen with dense, rounded growth, thriving in any soil or situation. There are good variegated forms, but their colour is not so bright in heavy shade. Propagation is by 15–20 cm (6–8 in) cuttings taken in the autumn and set out in open
2·5 m (8 ft) beds. Layers also root readily.

Camellia

(8 ft) Not planted nearly enough, these magnificent woodland plants prefer an acid soil, but are more tolerant of lime than the rhododendrons, and quite as hardy. Side-shade or dappled over-head shade is best and, as with the rhododendrons, mulching is important, especially when the plants are exposed to full sunlight, or the soil is liable to dry out. Air layering is a very convenient method of propagation, otherwise 10 cm (4 in) cuttings may be taken in August and September, and set in a shaded frame. Profes-sionally, they are usually grown from small leaf-bud cuttings. There are numerous fine varieties, some of the best being in the *japonica* section: 'Adolphe Audusson', a deep red; 'Apollo', rose red; 'Elegans', peach; 'Jupiter', scarlet; 'Lady Clare', pink; 'Nagasaki', pink with white marbling; and 'Tricolor', white and carmine streaks. In the *reticulata* section: 'Captain Rawes', carmine pink; and 'Mary Williams', crimson. In the *williamsii* section: 'Donation', orchid pink; and 'J. C. Williams', phlox pink. Among the hybrids, there are: 'Cornish Snow', white and 'Inspiration', deep pink. For massing, they may be planted 1 m (3 ft) apart.

Viburnum acerifolium

(7 ft) A useful shrub for fronting dark evergreens of the *Buxus* type. The specific name refers to the deciduous maple-like foliage which turns a rich crimson in the autumn. It does well in any soil type. Propagation may be achieved by cuttings which should be about 5 cm (2 in) long, either heeled or cut below a node, and taken during the summer. Alternatively, layering may be carried out before autumn; the buried portion of the layered shoot is best given a slight twist about 15 cm (6 in) from the tip. Plant 60 m (24 in) apart.

Osmanthus heterophyllus

Of similar appearance to the holly, with its glossy, dark green, spiny leaves, and tiny fragrant white flowers in the autumn, this evergreen thrives in any soil, and makes a dense screen. There are several good named variegations. It may be propagated by cuttings of side-shoots taken in September, or by layering in the autumn. In the latter case, a tongue should be cut 15–20 cm (6–8 in) from a shoot tip, which is pegged down firmly. For a dense cover, plant 75 cm (30 in) apart.

Symphytum peregrinum

7 ft) Comfrey survives in any soil or situation. It is rather coarse in habit, but very useful for rapidly clothing waste areas. A

HEIGHT

2 m (7 ft)

herbaceous plant, with large leaves and summer-long flowers which open rose pink and later turn blue. For propagation it may be divided in the autumn, and planted 1 m (3 ft) apart.

Rubus odoratus

A vigorous, deciduous, thornless bramble with red fruits, of tall, upright growth, with large, velvety palmate leaves and showy, fragrant flowers during the summer. It grows well in any soil, and is normally propagated by division. Plant at 1 m (3 ft).

Rubus spectabilis

A similar bramble, but prickly and slightly less tall, this very accommodating shrub has showy, fragrant, bright pink flowers in the spring, and edible orange berries. It is propagated either by division or by removing the suckers. Plant at 1 m (3 ft).

Taxus baccata 'Dovastonii'

1·7 m (6 ft)

The West Felton yew, remarkable for its low-growing, wide-spreading horizontal branch system and pendant branchlets. Eventually it needs a large area to spread, and if it grows too tall it may be stopped by removing the leading shoot. It is propagated by shoot cuttings taken in July and kept shaded. For a quick ground cover, plant at 1 m (3 ft) spacing.

Ribes alpinum

A deciduous currant bush, not noted for its flowers or berries, but useful because it retains its dense habit well when deeply shaded. It grows in any soil, and is propagated by 15–20 cm (6–8 in) cuttings taken in the autumn and set out in open sandy beds. Plant 60 cm (24 in) apart.

Symphoricarpos

The snowberries, thicket-forming deciduous shrubs useful for poor, dark corners. They grow in all types of soil, and may be kept tidy by cutting back. There are several species and varieties. Propagation is by division, or by cuttings of firm shoots 20 cm (8 in) long, which will root in open sandy beds. Plants may be spaced at 75 cm (30 in).

Cimicifuga

1·5 m (5 ft)

Very hardy herbaceous perennials, these shade plants prefer a moist, lime-free soil. There are several species and varieties, all with handsome divided leaves and white flowers. Propagation is by division in the spring; they may be planted 75 cm (30 in) apart.

Sarcococca confusa

A dense, vigorously spreading evergreen shrub that succeeds best in a moderately rich well-drained soil. The very fragrant white flowers open around Christmas and last all winter. Propagation may be achieved by 10 cm (4 in) cuttings taken in July and set in a shaded frame or, alternatively, harder cuttings may be taken in the autumn. Planting distance around 1·5 m (5 ft).

Ligularia dentata

A herbaceous perennial with huge, kidney-shaped leaves and showy orange flowers in July and August. The variety 'Desdemona' has purple leaves. Propagation is by division in the spring. Plants are best spaced about 60 cm (24 in) apart, on a moist site to the front of woodland.

Hydrangea

There are numerous species and varieties, all plants for the woodland edge, giving valuable late summer and autumn flowering colour. They need an acid soil to retain blue colouring, with the exception of *H. villosa* which retains its colour in a limy soil. 'Bluewave' is one of the best blue lacecaps for the woodland. For propagation, cuttings of 10 cm (4 in) tips taken at a node will strike readily in pots during late summer. Alternatively, shoots may be layered in the autumn. Plants may be set 75 cm (30 in) apart.

(4 ft)

Lonicera nitida

This evergreen bush honeysuckle is often used for hedges, a hardy plant thriving in all soils. The variety 'Baggessen's Gold' has yellow leaves. For ground cover under trees, bushes should be planted about 45 cm (18 in) apart. Propagation is by 30 cm (12 in) cuttings taken in the autumn, and set out in open, sandy beds.

Arundinaria fortunei

A dwarf bamboo which spreads vigorously and invasively, forming an impenetrable thicket. For some sites it can be very useful, but such places should be selected with care. It has attractive zig-zag green stems and variegated leaves. Propagation is simply a matter of division in the spring. Plant 1 m (3 ft) apart.

Gaultheria shallon

A very vigorous evergreen for lime-free soils. It forms a rapid cover and can be invasive, but is ideal for some confined patches of woodland. Plant at 1 m (3 ft) spacing. Propagation is by division in the spring, when the new growths are about 5–10 cm (2–4 in) high.

(4 ft)

HEIGHT

Rodgersia aesculifolia

1·1 m (4 ft)

Herbaceous perennials ideally suited to peaty soil in dappled shade at the woodland edge, where there is some shelter from the wind. The sculptural compound leaves are up to 45 cm (18 in) across, each horse chestnut-like leaflet measuring about 25 cm (10 in) long. Large white flower clusters are produced in mid summer. Planting may be at near 1 m (3 ft) spacing. The rodgersias may be propagated by division in the spring.

Rodgersia podophylla

Slightly smaller than *R. aesculifolia*, and with yellowish-white flower clusters, but suitable for the same sort of site. Propagation is identical. Space about 75 cm (30 in) apart.

Rodgersia tabularis

The smallest of the three bronze leafs, but similar in habits and requirements, it may also be planted at about a 75 cm (30 in) spacing, and propagation is identical.

Mahonia aquifolium

1·1 m (3 ft)

Thriving in situations where most other plants would fail, and enjoying alkaline soils, the Oregon grape has glossy dark ever-green leaves, and globular clusters of yellow flowers in the spring. It may be kept lightly clipped back to encourage a dense habit. Propagation is by division in the spring, or seed may be sown if this is available. Plants should be spaced about 60 cm (24 in) apart.

Daphne pontica

A pretty little wide-spreading evergreen shrub with bright, glossy leaves and fragrant greenish flowers in April and May. It enjoys a good, deep loam, whether this be acid or limy. A plant that looks best at the front of a woodland group. It is usually propagated from seed. Plant 75 cm (30 in) apart.

Polygonum campanulatum

One of the best spreading polygonums for the woodland garden, with panicles of pinkish-white flowers in the summer. It is not likely to get out of hand like the wretched *P. cuspidatum*, with zig-zag, blotchy stems. It may be divided in autumn or spring, and should be planted at a spacing of about 60 cm (24 in).

Viburnum davidii

0·90 m (3 ft)

An evergreen shrub that forms dense ground cover with glossy, dark green, spreading mounds. The flowers are small and incon-

Viburnum davidii. This evergreen carpeting shrub has small flowers followed by bright blue fruits which last throughout the winter.

า (3 ft) spicuous, but the bright blue showy fruits persist throughout the winter. It does well in any soil, and should be planted at a 45 cm (18 in) spacing. Propagation is by 5–7 cm (2–3 in) cuttings with a heel or cut below a node, taken during July and August and set directly into small pots beneath a frame.

Arundinaria vagans

A dwarf bamboo that is less invasive than *A. fortunei*, and well behaved beneath trees. It has a bright, attractive green colour. Propagation is by simple division during the spring, the pieces replanted 60 cm (24 in) apart.

Sarcococca ruscifolia

A spreading evergreen that thrives in any soil but especially appreciates lime, the fragrant white flowers open around Christmas. It should be planted at a 65 cm (26 in) spacing. Propagation is by division in the spring, or cuttings may be taken in July, using 5–10 cm (2–4 in) side-shoots, set in a shaded frame.

Ruscus aculeatus

Butcher's broom, a creeping evergreen shrub which will thrive in
า (2⅔ ft) any soil, being especially useful in dry, densely shaded spots. It

HEIGHT

0·80 m (2⅔ ft)

forms thick clumps of attractive, glossy green foliage, with bright red berries. It may be planted at a 60 cm (24 in) spacing, and is propagated by division in the spring.

Skimmia japonica

A dense, rounded, evergreen shrub with leathery leaves, white flowers in April and bright red berries. It grows well on acid or alkaline soils. The variety 'Foremanii' has broader leaves and large clusters of brilliant red fruits. 'Fragrans' has a broad, densely-spreading form, and bears panicles of fragrant white flowers. Plants may be set 60 cm (24 in) apart. Cuttings of side-shoots may be taken in the autumn, and autumn layering is also effective. The layered portion should be only 5–10 cm (2–4 in) long, and the shoot should not be cut or twisted.

0·75 m (2½ ft)

Skimmia japonica, an evergreen shrub with leathery leaves and white flowers in spring followed by bright red berries.

HT

(2½ ft)

Taxus baccata 'Repandens'

A prostrate yew which forms a wide-spreading bush of fresh, dark green foliage. 'Repandens Aurea' has gold tips to the branchlets, especially in the sun. Propagated by cuttings of terminal shoots taken in July and set in a shaded frame. For a quick cover, plant 75 cm (30 in) apart.

Lonicera pileata

An evergreen bush of dense, horizontal growth, especially useful for covering steep banks. It grows readily in any soil or site, in sun or shade. A honeysuckle not noted for its flowers, with small, bright green leaves. Planting may be at a spacing of 75 cm (30 in). Propagation is by 30 cm (12 in) tip cuttings taken in December and set in open beds, or shorter, heeled side-shoots taken in July and set in a frame.

(2½ ft)

Hypericum androsaemum

Tutsan makes an attractive, compact bush, covered with small yellow flowers during the summer, and red and black berries in the autumn. It grows well on any soil, and often seeds itself. Seed may be sown *in situ*, otherwise 15 cm (6 in) cuttings may be taken in the autumn and set out in open beds. Plant 60 cm (24 in) apart.

Rhododendron

The lower-growing species and varieties. Some of the best of the small woodland species are: *R. baileyi*, with small leaves and bright reddish-purple flowers in May; *R. bathyphyllum*, densely leaved, with crimson-spotted white flowers in late spring; *R. brachycarpum*, with pale yellow flowers in early summer; *R. caloxanthum*, with small, rounded leaves, becoming covered during April and May with yellow flowers which are scarlet-tipped in bud; *R. cephalanthum*, with heads of tiny white flowers in May; *R. citriniflorum*, with pink-tinged yellow flowers in April and May; *R. degronianum*, a compact, rounded bush with pale pink flowers in May; *R. fastigiatum*, of similar shape but with much smaller leaves and purple flowers in May; *R. glomerulatum*, with tiny leaves and pale mauve flowers throughout the spring; *R. gymnocarpum*, a compact shrub with thick, leathery leaves and dainty pale yellow flowers, marked with crimson, during April and May; *R. orthocladum*, with small, greyish leaves and masses of pale mauve flowers in April; *R. triplonaevium*, with reddish-downy young leaves and crimson-blotched white flowers in April and May; *R. valentinianum*, with small, rounded leaves and bright shining yellow flowers in April. There are numerous lower-growing

(2½ ft)

HEIGHT

0·65 m (2⅛ ft)

named hybrid varieties, some of the best of which are: 'April Chimes', mauve-pink, April; 'Arthur J. Ivens', pink, April; 'Arthur Osborne', blood red, June; 'Blue Diamond', lavender blue, April; 'Break of Day', orange-red, May; 'Britannia', crimson-scarlet, May; 'Burning Bush', tangerine red, May; 'Cilpinense', pinkish-white, March; 'Corona', coral pink, May; 'Cowslip', pale prim-rose, May; 'Dairy Maid', cream marked with crimson, May; 'Don-caster', crimson-scarlet, May; 'Elizabeth', dark red, April; 'Firetail', deep scarlet, May; 'Goblin', salmon pink, May; 'Golden Horn', orange-red, May; 'Goldsworth Orange', orange tinged with pink, June; 'Goldsworth Yellow', primrose, May; 'Hermes', yellow marked with pink, May; 'Humming Bird', carmine scarlet, April; 'Jamaica', deep orange, April; 'Kingcup', bright yellow, May; 'Lady Chamberlain', bright orange, May; 'Letty Edwards', yellow, May; 'Little Bert', crimson-scarlet, April; 'May Day', brilliant scarlet, May; 'Medusa', bright orange-red, May; 'Moon-stone', pink in bud, opening pale primrose, April; 'Mrs Mary Ashley', creamy pink, April; 'Nereid', salmon pink, May; 'Oud-jik's Sensation', bright pink, May; 'Penjerrick', creamy yellow,

0·60 m (2 ft)

April; 'Praecox', rose-purple, February; 'Racil', blush pink, April; 'Rubina', blood red, June; 'Saint Breward', lavender, April; 'Saint Tudy', lobelia blue, May; 'Songbird', violet, April; 'Sussex Bonfire', blood red, May; 'Tessa', purplish pink spotted with crimson, March; 'Valaspis', bright yellow, March; 'Vanessa', soft pink, June. They may be planted about 1 m (3 ft) apart.

Deciduous hybrid azaleas include the Ghent hybrids with nar-row, long tubed flowers, the Knap Hill hybrids and the Mollis azaleas, both with large, trumpet-shaped, scentless flowers, the Occidentale and the Rustica hybrids with scented flowers, all flowering in May, and all eminently suitable for large woodland gardens. They are usually planted at a spacing of 1 m (3 ft).

Of more compact size are the evergreen hybrid Kurume azaleas. They are best massed in dappled shade—a clearing or glade adjacent to woodland is the ideal spot, leaving the darker shaded areas to the tougher-leaved rhododendrons. At Windsor Great Park the Kurume azaleas are given a light clipping with shears shortly after flowering. This keeps them compact, shortens leading shoots and encourages masses of flowering side-shoots—it also removes dead-heads and prevents seed-setting. In that famous garden, they also receive an annual fairly thick top-dressing of leaf mould which feeds the plants, retains the all-important moisture, and helps to check weeds. As is the case with all rhododendrons and azaleas, they are notoriously shallow-rooted, and forking over

0·55 m (1⅞ ft)

the ground beneath them is not a good idea. They may be propa-

HT

n (1⅔ft) gated using 5 cm (2 in) shoots of the current season's growth taken with a heel, ideally during July and August, and inserted in a shaded frame, using a sandy compost. When two or three years old, they may be planted out 70 cm (28 in) apart. Some of the most popular Kurume varieties are: 'Assa-Gasumi', rose-pink; 'Hana-Asobi', red; 'Kimigayo', creamy pink; 'Kirin', bright rose; 'Kiritsubo', crimson; 'Rashomon', scarlet; 'Suga-no-ito', mauve-pink; 'Takasayo', pink; and 'Ukamuse', vermilion.

Ruscus hypoglossum
Similar to but dwarfer than butcher's broom, this creeping evergreen shrub thrives on any soil or site, forming a thick cover with its broad, spreading clumps. The leaves are an attractively glossy green, and it bears cherry-like berries. Propagation is by division in the spring, and planting at a 50 cm (20 in) spacing.

Luzula maxima 'Variegata'
A thick, grass-like cover, useful for dry shade or on steep banks where mowing is difficult. The creeping rootstocks may be

n (1⅔ft) divided in the spring and planted 40 cm apart.

Mertensia virginica
Virginian cowslip is a spreading herb with attractive foliage which dies down in the autumn. Purple-blue flowers are produced in May and June. Seed may be sown as soon as it is ripe, otherwise the plants may be divided in the autumn. Plant at 30 cm (12 in).

Leucothoe fontanesiana
An evergreen covering shrub for lime-free soils. It has arching stems wreathed in white flowers during May, and pointed leathery green leaves which become richly coloured red, purple and bronze in the autumn. It should be planted at a 45 cm (18 in) spacing. Propagation is by summer cuttings of 5–10 cm (2–4 in) heeled side-shoots, alternatively by layering in the autumn, in which case the shoot to be layered should be twisted 15 cm (6 in) from the tip and pegged down into a peaty soil.

Sarcococca humilis
A densely spreading shrub with glossy, evergreen foliage. The very fragrant white flowers, which appear during the winter, are followed by black berries. It grows in any soil, but prefers lime. Plant 60 cm (24 in) apart; propagate by division in the spring. It should not be used beneath newly planted trees, for the matted root

n (1½ft) system would compete too fiercely for surface moisture.

Euonymus radicans 'Variegatus'. This particular form, with its silver and gold markings, stands out well in a shaded situation.

Vancouveria hexandra

0·45 m (1½ ft) An attractive creeping perennial forming hummocks of fern-like deciduous foliage with dainty white flowers in May. It enjoys cool, shady situations in a peaty soil. Plants may be divided in spring or autumn, and should be planted 45 cm (18 in) apart.

Euonymus radicans

A prostrate, evergreen, shrubby scrambler, rooting as it goes and slowly reaching a metre or two (3–6 ft) across. The type has dark green leaves, but there are many good variegated forms. 'Variegatus' is very bright with silver and gold markings, and stands out well in shaded situations. Planting espacement may be about 60 cm (24 in). When the plants are spreading well, rooted portions may be removed for replanting, otherwise cuttings of heeled side-shoots can be taken in July and rooted in a sandy, shaded frame.

Tiarella cordifolia

For quick ground cover in cool spots, the foam flower is a useful wide-spreading perennial for the woodland. The starry white flowers appear from April to June, and the foliage turns a reddish 0·40 m (1⅓ ft) bronze in the autumn. The variety 'Purpurea' has bronze-purple leaves throughout the summer, and rose-pink flowers. It should be planted at a 50 cm (20 in) spacing, and propagation is by division of the spreading stolons.

Petasites albus

Forms a rampant and invasive cover in moist woodland, growing rapidly in any soil. It has attractive, fine foliage and white flowers in the spring, and looks particularly well by the waterside, but its site should be selected with caution. Plant 60 cm (24 in) apart, and propagate by division.

Geranium

These accommodating hardy perennials are indispensable for difficult places, and useful for covering ground temporarily before the slower growing shrubs have filled their allotted spaces. They are usually planted 45 cm (18 in) apart, and may be propagated by division in the spring or autumn. The most useful are: G. *endressii*, a very rapid ground coverer which prefers a cool, well-drained site among shrubs—a pretty plant with pink flowers in summer and autumn; 'Claridge Druce', with large magenta flowers, will stand heavy shade; 'Rose Clair' has white flowers veined with crimson; 'Wargrave Pink' has scented leaves and clear pink flowers throughout the summer; 'Johnson's Blue' is free-flowering, bright blue veined with red; G. *macrorrhizum* is a very rapid spreader for cool situations, with scented foliage and red or purple flowers from May to July—in spite of being deciduous it maintains a good cover with its mass of rooted stems; 'Russell Prichard' endures only light shade and is also deciduous, but makes a grey-green summer carpet by throwing out shoots annually from its firm crown—dotted with magenta flowers throughout the season; 'Buxton's Blue' stands light shade only, and bears large violet-blue flowers throughout summer and autumn.

Trachystemon orientalis

This is a spreading perennial with numerous purple-blue flowers which usually appear before the large and hairy, weed-smothering leaves, in the spring. It may be propagated by division in the autumn, and planted at a 50 cm (20 in) spacing.

Vinca major

The large periwinkle thrives in any soil, though it may take a few years to become well established, and eventually will start to spread rapidly. It has arching shoots, and purple-blue flowers in the spring. The cream-blotched form 'Variegata' is slower to spread

89

0·30 m (1 ft)

than the green type. It may be planted at a spacing of 45 cm (18 in), and is propagated by division in early spring. Alternatively, 5–10 cm (2–4 in) cuttings of shoot tips taken in October and placed in a frame will root readily.

Hypericum calycinum

Rose of Sharon, a vigorous, spreading, shrubby evergreen for any soil, with gorgeous golden flowers from June to September. It may be clipped in March to retain a neat habit. Plants should be spaced at 40 cm (16 in). Propagation is by division in spring or autumn, or heeled side-shoots may be rooted in July. Bushy plants are usually produced quickly from three cuttings placed together in a pot.

Dicentra formosa

The bleeding heart is useful for the woodland border. Some varieties are: 'Adrian Bloom', with finely cut leaves and plentiful crimson, heart-shaped flowers from April to June; 'Album', with ferny foliage and white flowers during the summer, is long-flowered in shady spots provided the soil does not dry out; 'Bountiful' has purple-pink flowers from spring to autumn, and seeds itself readily. Propagation is normally by division in the early spring, or the roots may be cut into short lengths and planted out. Plants are spaced at about 45 cm (18 in).

25 cm (10 in)

Vancouveria planipetala

The redwood ivy, an attractive, creeping, woodland evergreen with white or lavender-tinged flowers in May. Plants may be divided in spring or autumn, and should be planted about 40 cm (16 in) apart.

Gaylussacia brachycera

A shrub which forms a thick, leathery, evergreen mat on lime-free, well-drained loamy soil, with tiny white flowers in May and June, followed by bluish, edible berries. Plants should be spaced at 55 cm (22 in). Propagation can be achieved by tip cuttings taken in the summer and set in a shaded frame, alternatively, rooted 'Irishman's cuttings' are often available.

Pachysandra terminalis

Forms a very effective, rapid cover in lime-free soil, with attractive light green rosettes of evergreen foliage. Plants need a 45 cm (18 in) spacing, but 'Variegata' forms a less dense cover, and should be planted closer, say 35 cm (14 in). Propagation is easily achieved by division in the spring or autumn.

22 cm (9 in)

Pachysandra terminalis has attractive light green rosettes of evergreen foliage.

Symphytum grandiflorum

n (9 in) Makes a prolific close-growing cover beneath shrubs and on awk-ward banks, a leafy perennial whose flowers in spring and early summer are red-tipped when in bud, opening yellow. Plants may be divided in the autumn and spaced 45 cm (18 in) apart.

Polygonum affine 'Lowndes Variety'

A spreading perennial with impressive, brilliantly pink flower spikes from July to October. The carpet of leaves colours in the autumn, dies and turns brown, but remains as a cover over winter. It will grow in any soil type, but not in very dry or shady places; the woodland edge is the ideal site. Propagation is by division in spring or autumn, and plants should be spaced at 35 cm (14 in).

Vaccinium vitis-idaea

Mountain cranberry is more shade-bearing than the bilberry with which it associates. In Scotland it is a remnant of the ancient pine forests which once clothed the uplands, when it thrived in the light shade as an under-storey plant. Creeping and evergreen, with glossy, dark green box-like leaves, and red, acid-tasting berries, it

1 (8 in) forms a close shrubby cover for lime-free soil when spaced at 35 cm

(14 in). Propagation is achieved by cuttings of short side-shoots taken with a heel during the summer, and set individually into small pots, using a sandy compost.

Rubus tricolor

An evergreen, thornless, creeping bramble with bright red berries, very vigorous in any soil type, and one of the few plants that will survive in the heavy shade cast by beech trees. It may spread nearly 2 m (6½ ft) in one season, and this is a convenient plant spacing to adopt for a quick cover. Propagation is simply a matter of removing rooted stems.

Gaultheria procumbens

A vigorous, hardy, shrubby evergreen cover for lime-free soils, with scented foliage and white or pink flowers in July and August, followed by red berries. Plants should be divided in the spring, and planted 60 cm (24 in) apart.

Petasites fragrans

19 cm (7 in) The winter heliotrope, deciduous, with white vanilla-scented flowers appearing in February before the leaves. In light shade it forms a close cover with its large leaves in any soil, but it can be invasive. It may be propagated by division in the autumn and planted at a 45 cm (18 in) spacing.

Bergenia

A very useful multi-purpose plant to link sun and shade; for buffering invasive spreaders, and to contrast with angled leaf forms. The oval, glossy, dark green, fleshy leaves turn coppery red in the winter. Two of the best varieties are 'Ballawley', the largest, with pink flowers in March and April and 'Evening Glow', with dark crimson flowers appearing late. They grow in most types of soil, and should be planted 45 cm (18 in) apart. Propagation is by division in spring or autumn.

Cardamine trifolia

For any soil in damp, shady situations, it forms a dark evergreen mat of pretty three-lobed leaves, becoming covered with small white flowers in the spring. Propagation is by division in the autumn, and plants may be set at a 40 cm (16 in) spacing.

Epimedium

18 cm (7 in) Creeping perennials which like a loamy, peaty soil. They bear dainty aquilegia-like flowers in the spring and handsome, slowly

HT

(7 in)

spreading foliage. Some of the best varieties and species are: *E. perralderianum*, deciduous, with bright yellow flowers, for a 45 cm (18 in) spacing; *E. pinnatum* 'Colchicum', evergreen with yellow flowers, also for a 45 cm (18 in) spacing; *E. rubrum*, deciduous with pink flowers, to be spaced at 40 cm (16 in); *E. versicolor* 'Sulphureum', deciduous, with yellow flowers, also for a 40 cm (16 in) spacing; and *E. warleyense* is deciduous with a red and yellow flower, to be planted at a 35 cm (14 in) spacing. In all cases, dead leaves should be trimmed off in January for the flowers to be seen at their best. They are propagated by division during July and August.

Ajuga

The bugles are perennial herbs which carpet moist woods, with rounded, oblong leaves and blue flower spikes from April to July. The best species for the woodland garden are *E. pyramidalis* and *E. reptans*, and the latter has several named varieties, among them 'Variegata' and 'Multicolor', which have pink and white variegated leaves, and 'Atropurpurea' with purple leaves. All may be planted at about a 40 cm (16 in) spacing, and may readily be propagated by division.

Oxalis oregana

(7 in)

An American wood sorrel that also thrives in Britain, and forms a vigorous weed-proof cover in cool woodland conditions. The dainty rose pink flowers are about 2·5 cm (1 in) long, and very pretty in April and May. Propagation is by division of the rhizomes, and plants should be spaced at about 40 cm (16 in).

Asperula odorata

Woodruff is a British perennial herb often found wild on chalky soils, though it will grow on other types, and is especially rampant in sandy situations. In the semi-shade of light woodland and among damp, dead leaves, woodruff thrives and forms a drift of starry, fragrant white flowers in May and June. Propagation is by division in the spring or early summer, and planting may be at a 40 cm (16 in) spacing.

Vinca minor

The small periwinkle is an evergreen that thrives on any soil, and is quicker to spread than the large periwinkle *V. major*. The typical species has purple-blue flowers from April throughout the summer, but a carpet formed of mixed varieties is very effective. Some of the best are: 'Alba', with white flowers; 'Bowles Variety', with single sky-blue flowers, and the most vigorous in woodland

(6 in)

conditions; 'Multiplex' has double dark purple flowers; 'Variegata' has leaves marked with creamy yellow and is not as vigorous as the others. They may be propagated by division in spring or autumn, and should be planted 45 cm (18 in) apart.

Alchemilla mollis

Lady's mantle is a perennial herb with large soft hairy leaves, well covered with small greenish flowers in the summer. It makes an unusual patch for the dappled shade at the woodland edge. It grows well in any soil, and usually seeds itself freely. Seed is, in any case, the best method of propagation. Planting should be at about 45 cm (18 in) spacing.

Alchemilla alpina

The mountain lady's mantle is to be found wild in the Scottish Highlands. With its attractive round leaves and small green flowers it forms a mat on well-drained soil, in sun or partial shade, and is ideal to cover the front of the woodland border. Propagation is easiest by seed, and planting should be at a 40 cm (16 in) spacing.

Lamium

The dead nettles, creeping perennials which form reliable carpets in the woodland garden. Their requirements vary, but all may be propagated readily by division in autumn or spring. As they are shallow rooting, they may easily be removed and kept within bounds. Some of the most useful species or varieties are: *L. galeobdolon*, the yellow archangel, so called from the winged shape of the tiny yellow flowers which appear in clusters during the summer—it should be spaced at 45 cm (18 in) and is suitable for a light, limy soil; its variety 'Variegatum' with white marked leaves, good for light calcareous soils and especially suitable for interplanting with bulbs as it does not make so dense a cover, also to be planted at 45 cm (18 in); *L. garganicum* with red flowers, and *L. orvala* with purplish flowers both do well in poor, dry soils, and should be planted 40 cm (16 in) apart; *L. maculatum* has larger leaves than the others, each leaf bearing a conspicuous silver-white stripe which contrasts with the dark green margins. It is a vigorous colonizer which enjoys a moist soil and spreads densely in the more open places. A spacing of 45 cm (18 in) is about right.

Arctostaphylos uva-ursi

The bear grape likes a deep well-drained lime-free loam, where it will rapidly make a shrubby, evergreen cover with glossy round
leaves, pinkish spring flowers, and brilliant red berries. Propaga-

tion is either by division in the autumn, or by cuttings 6–7 cm (2–3 in) long, taken in September and struck in a closed frame, using a sandy compost. Plants should be spaced at about 35 cm (14 in) apart.

Asarum europaeum

Makes a thick carpet of lush, glossy green, kidney-shaped leaves, for any soil in shady places. Plants may be divided in the spring, and planted 50 cm (20 in) apart.

Oxalis acetosella

The wood sorrel, a dainty little British perennial which forms a mat of yellowish green clover-like leaves through which bulbs may grow. The flowers are white, veined with lilac, and appear in April and May. The variety 'Rosea' has rose-coloured flowers with purple veins. Propagation is by division in the early spring, and plants should be set 35 m (14 in) apart.

Cornus canadensis

So unlike the other dogwoods, it may sometimes be found listed under its own genus *Chamaepericlymenum*. It can be invasive, spreading by nearly a metre (3 ft) in one year, but it makes a

Cornus canadensis. Ideal for planting beneath large trees. Its starry white flowers are followed by red berries.

HEIGHT

13 cm (5 in)

magnificent carpet beneath large trees in damp, lime-free soil. The starry white flowers are followed by red berries, and there are bright autumnal tints before the leaves are shed. Propagation may be achieved by division in the early spring, and planting should be at a spacing of 60 cm (24 in).

Acaena microphylla

A compact, ground-hugging evergreen perennial with showy crimson flower bracts in the summer. It grows in any ordinary well-drained soil and, being tolerant of quite heavy shade, does well under conifers. Seed germinates readily, otherwise plants may be divided in autumn or early spring, and spaced at approximately 35 cm (14 in) intervals.

Omphalodes verna

Blue-eyed Mary, a valuable little carpeting perennial which increases rapidly by runners, and becomes covered with white-throated blue flowers in the spring. For any soil in light woodland, it may be planted at a 45 cm (18 in) spacing, and propagated by division in autumn or spring.

Waldsteinia ternata

12 cm (5 in)

For the woodland edge, an evergreen mat-forming perennial which grows in any soil, but takes a couple of seasons to become established. It has dark green strawberry-like foliage, and dainty yellow spring flowers. Plants may be divided in the spring, and planted out about 30 cm (12 in) apart.

Nepeta hederacea

Ground ivy is fine in wild woodland, but may be too invasive for the garden. Its variety 'Variegata' is not so vigorous, and does not make a heavy cover, but dapples the ground with its attractive leaves. For propagation the creeping stems may be removed with roots attached, or cuttings of soft tips may be taken during the summer. Plants should be set 80 cm (32 in) apart.

Fragaria indica

Possibly the most rapid runner of all, once it is firmly established, it may spread up to 2 m (6½ ft) in one season and forms a weed-proof mat of greenery, covered in late summer and autumn with tiny red strawberries. It thrives in most situations, dry or moist, and may be propagated like cultivated strawberries by removing rooted runners, or pegging them to root into small pots sunk in the ground.

11 cm (4 in)

Planting should be at a spacing of just over a metre (3 ft).

HT

(4 in)

Helxine soleirolii

Mind-your-own-business is a vigorous perennial ideally suited to carpeting cool, moist places, and scrambling about among shady rocks. The small, glossy evergreen leaves may become blackened by severe frosts, but the plant will usually recover. Propagation is by soft tip cuttings taken in the summer and set in a shaded frame. Planting should be at a 45 cm (18 in) spacing.

5
Dot Plants:
Bulbs, Climbers and Ferns

These are the dot plants—the finishing touches; the sculptural form that accentuates and complements; the bright splash of colour to draw the eye; that little surprise around the corner which makes the visitor stop and admire. The barrier plants that prevent two vigorous runners quarrelling; the exclamation mark that raises the eyebrows towards some special vista; the leaf-plant included solely for its colour, to brighten, or soften, or blend.

Bulbs, of course, must be introduced into the herbaceous ground-layer almost as a matter of routine. Bluebells and snow-drops may sometimes seem a little hackneyed through over-use, but it is difficult to imagine a woodland garden without them. Of slightly more refined taste, but just as trouble-free, are the anemones, both the blue and the white kinds, and these may be introduced freely into any scheme; they look equally good to the front, or as a splash of quiet colour in the shade.

Lily of the valley and the similar *Galax* and *Maianthemum* are also best included as an afterthought, into places where their sometimes sparse leaves can serve to bolster any of the covering plants which are not forming too close a mat.

This chapter lists a selection of plants which fall into these categories. Personal preference will play a large part in their choice; any plant may be used if it pleases its owner and is able to grow and thrive in the conditions offered, and such a list, however long, can never be complete.

Acanthus

Handsome plants of upright, spire-like form, about 1 m (3 ft) tall. They love woodland conditions, although the foxglove-like but spiny flowers really need the sun for full development. They may be planted 45 cm (18 in) apart, and propagated by division in autumn or early spring. They often set seed, and this may some-

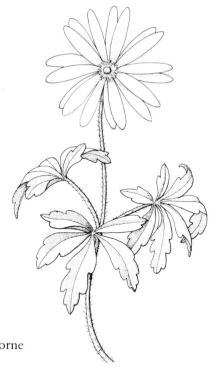

Anemone blanda. Deep blue flowers are borne between February and April.

times be sown successfully merely by scattering *in situ*. Two suit-able species are:

A. mollis: Has soft, 60 cm (24 in) long heart–shaped leaves, and spikes of white or rose flowers in the late summer; and

A. spinosus: Has huge, thistly, spiny leaves, with very freely borne, taller spikes of flowers.

Anemone

There are many wind flowers which do well in woodland and semi-woodland conditions, though not all are readily obtainable from nurseries. Those listed here look most natural in the garden, are usually available, and normally planted as tubers, though they may be propagated from seed which often germinates well.

A. apennina: Takes eagerly to naturalizing. The 4 cm (1½ in) wide flowers in March are of a clear blue colour which lasts well in woodland shade. There are also pink, white and double-flowered forms. For a massed effect, space at 15 cm (6 in).

A. blanda: Has 7·5 cm (3 in) wide flowers of deep blue, opening as early as February and blooming until April. The variety 'Atrocoerulea' has darker, royal blue flowers. Both the species and the variety are less shade-loving than *A. apennina*, and should be sited in a sunny, sheltered spot on the woodland edge, 15 cm (6 in) apart.

A. canadensis: A tall, woodland anemone found wild over much of North America, with starry white flowers in May, on branching 50 cm (20 in) stems. Plants should be spaced at 35 cm (14 in).

A. nemorosa: The wood anemone found wild in British woods, with dainty white pink-tinged flowers in March. There are several good varieties, among them: 'Alba Plena', a double white; 'Alleni' and 'Blue Bonnet', both with large, pale blue flowers; 'Rosea', pink; 'Robinsoniana', with large lavender-blue flowers; and 'Royal Blue', which is accurately named. All may be spaced at 15 cm (6 in) for massed planting.

Aquilegia

Columbine. There are many varieties, some of which enjoy shade, and others which do not. The McKana hybrids are excellent and colourful as a summer-long link between ground cover and the taller shrubs. They set seed prolifically and may be sown *in situ* every year. When newly planted they may be spaced at 30 cm (12 in).

Astilbe

The many varieties with their colourful plumes in late summer are well known in association with the water garden, but all are at their showiest in a woodland setting where the soil is moist and deep. Propagation is by division in the spring, and plants may be set at about 45 cm (18 in) apart. Some of the best varieties are: 'Bressingham Beauty', pink, 80 cm (32 in) tall; 'Fanal', ruby red, 75 cm (30 in) tall; 'Irrlicht', white, 60 cm (24 in) tall; 'Red Sentinel', brick red, 60 cm (24 in) tall; 'Venus', deep pink, 1 m (3 ft) tall; and 'Fire', salmon-red, 60 cm (24 in) tall.

Chionodoxa

Of great value as a woodland naturalizer, because the exquisite blue flowers appear in early spring before other vegetation has had a chance to grow, and, by the end of spring, the delicate snowdrop-like leaves have withered and disappeared completely for another year. They may be planted 10 cm (4 in) apart.

C. gigantea: The flowers are larger than the other species, and the colour has more than a hint of lilac. There is a white-flowered form 'Alba'.

C. luciliae: The intensely sky-blue flowers, usually 5 or 6 to each bulb and measuring 2·5 cm (1 in) across, are borne 15 cm (6 in) off the ground. There is a pink variety, 'Rosea'.

C. sardensis: Of similar size but earlier flowering than *luciliae*, with bright gentian-blue flowers.

Climbers

Ivy, honeysuckle and wild clematis are the three climbers that most frequently occur wild in British woods. Ivy, of course, can often be put to good use in the woodland garden. The Irish ivy, *Hedera hibernica*, rarely climbs, and so is excellent as a ground cover plant in areas of dense shade where little else but some of the ferns would grow. All the ivies will cover ground, and the variegated ones grow perhaps less vigorously than the wild green kinds, but normally they will climb when they get the chance. The large-leaved variegated types, *H. dentata* 'Variegata' and *H. helix* 'Sagit-taefolia' are prolific and vigorous—ideal for rapidly converting a wire fence into a solid, wind-proof hedge. The best small-leaved varieties are: 'Gold Heart', each leaf bearing a central yellow blotch, with a very handsome general effect; 'Angularis Aurea', with medium-sized leaves of all-over yellow; 'Glacier', with a silver and green variegation; and 'Marginata Rubra', whose leaf-margins are a yellowish-white in the summer, but turn a deep rosy red in the autumn. When used as ground-cover, they are usually planted about 30 cm (15 in) apart.

Ivies can swamp small garden trees if allowed to rampage on them, although they can do little harm to large specimens. Indeed, after many years as a forester I cannot recall ever seeing a timber tree that had beyond doubt been harmed by ivy. It is a different matter where honeysuckle is concerned; young trees can be seriously constricted and distorted by this beautiful climber, for the twining stems do not have the ivy's 'give' to enable them to expand as the tree grows. Honeysuckle is best used, therefore, as a back-drop, or to cover some unsightly object—a domestic fuel tank, perhaps, for the vigorous kinds such as *Lonicera japonica* 'Halliana', whose fragrant white and gold flowers appear rather sparsely but over a long period, seem to thrive on the drips and fumes from the fuel-oil.

There are many excellent varieties, especially *L. periclymenum* 'Belgica', the early Dutch, and *L. periclymenum* 'Serotina', the late Dutch honeysuckles. They both have deliciously fragrant purplish-red and yellow flowers, 'Belgica' from June to July, and 'Serotina' from August to September, and both are varieties of the wild British species. The hybrid *L. × tellmanniana* is a vigorously rapid grower that prefers shade, but the large coppery-yellow flowers, though borne in great profusion, are scentless. These honeysuckles will easily cover an area 3 m (10 ft) square.

Wild clematis is not a plant to introduce into the garden. If it likes the site it will take over the woodland edge completely, and do harm to the bordering shrubs. Neither are the large-flowered clematis hybrids often very successful in wild garden conditions, for they are plants which prefer a site of their own, and woodland competition is a little too fierce.

There are several smaller-flowered species, however, which are ideally suited to this environment, either to scramble through trees that are sparsely branched enough to admit them, or to cover rough banks or old stumps. There is a great temptation, if one has a dead or dying tree, to use it as a support for a climbing plant; but trees, like people, seldom die of old age—there is always a reason—and if there is an infection such as honey fungus, then that dead tree is going to infect all the others around it. A much wiser step is to dig the dead tree out and, if possible, disinfect the immediate area before replanting. (There are notes on this in Chapter 7.) In the forest, there is a strong case for allowing dead wood to remain as a source of food and a breeding ground for many different creatures. In the woodland garden, however, this would be carrying conservation to dangerous lengths.

Because wild clematis grows on calcareous sites, it is frequently assumed that clematis in general need a limy soil, but this is not the case. All the species and varieties seem to do equally well on both acid and limy soils. *Clematis flammula* is an autumn-flowering species that takes readily to the woodland; it carries loose panicles of very fragrant, pure white, cross-shaped flowers. *C. orientalis* is another autumn flowerer, this time with bright yellow, nodding flowers, each with a purple centre. Another for the autumn is *C. rehderiana*, with pale yellow, bell-shaped flowers, and yet another yellow-flowered species is *C. tangutica*, which flowers in July. All these species will cover an area about 4·5 m (15 ft) square.

The well known spring-flowering *C. montana* is always reliable in semi-wild conditions, producing masses of fragrant, cross-shaped, pure white flowers, each 6–7 cm (2–3 in) wide. 'Rubens' is a rosy-purple flowered variety with purplish young leaves. A vigorous grower, not to say a rampager, *C. montana* tends to produce a great tangle that is difficult to deal with. Trimming back when needed should be done as soon as the flowering period is over and, in these semi-wild conditions, an overgrown specimen can usually be dealt with effectively merely by snipping through some of the main stems low down, and allowing the consequent dead wood and leaves to stay where they are. There is no danger here; they will soon become camouflaged beneath fresh growth, and will have decomposed almost completely within a few seasons. A well-grown plant is capable of covering an area 9 m (30 ft) square.

A specialized climber that can be of great value in some circumstances is the vine *Vitis coignetiae*, a hardy and vigorous grower that

Clematis montana. A very well-known climber, which grows vigorously and produces a mass of white, cross-shaped flowers.

may reach 25 m (83 ft) if the support is there. Its great value lies in the architectural quality of its huge leaves—each 30 cm (12 in) wide—and when used as a backdrop it can do remarkable things with perspective and scale. In a small garden it should be used with caution, but it has been introduced to great effect into tiny court-yard gardens in the town, and it may also be used as a ground-cover plant. The leaves turn brilliantly crimson and scarlet in the autumn.

By the nature of these climbing plants with their long, questing shoots, occasionally rooting as they come into contact with moist earth, layering and air layering are often the best methods of propagation. Clematis species may be grown also from internodal cuttings. By this method, a trailer is removed and cut immediately above every pair of buds that bear healthy leaves. The resultant cuttings are shortened to about 4–5 cm (1½–2 in) lengths and kept well shaded in a closed frame. The operation is best carried out in late spring and, in the case of *C. montana* at least, may be combined with annual pruning.

The ivies will also root from internodal, but more readily from nodal cuttings, their lengths depending on the distance between buds, and they may conveniently be set four or five together in a small pot, if there is enough propagating material available, as this method will produce bushy young plants.

Convallaria majalis

Lily of the valley, the sweetly scented flower that is at its best in moist woodland. For propagation, the crowns are lifted and divided in the autumn, and planting is at a spacing of 20–25 cm (8–10 in). 'Everest' is an improved variety, and an unusual choice is 'Rosea', with light pink flowers.

Cyclamen

These very beautiful little plants love a sheltered woodland spot where they can be left alone to thrive and multiply. They are not fussy about the soil type, though the planting position must be moist but well drained—in other words, the tubers do not like to stand in water, neither do they like to dry out. If the site does tend to be dry, they should be planted a little deeper, say at 10 cm (4 in) instead of 5 cm (2 in). An annual mulch of leaf mould will help to keep the moisture in during the summer months. They should be spaced about 20 cm (8 in) apart.

C. europaeum: Has fragrant, deep carmine flowers lasting from August into the autumn, and sometimes appearing again in the spring. The leaves are almost evergreen, and often have a silver-marked zone on the upper surface and a strong red tinge below. There is a fragrant, white-flowered variety, 'Album'.

C. neapolitanum: The flowers are pink with a deep carmine blotch, and are produced from July to November. The leaves are variable in size, shape and markings, but are always attractive, and form a carpet during the winter.

C. coum: The winter-flowering cyclamen, carmine with deep crimson spots, blooming from January to March. The leaves are rounded and usually dark green, but there are numerous varieties, many of which have silver markings. 'Roseum' has pale pink flowers; 'Album' has white flowers which, however, usually retain the crimson spots.

C. libanoticum: This species has fragrant flowers of a very pale rose pink, with a deep carmine central blotch. They open as early as February, followed by the young leaves which are white-zoned above and purple on the undersides. This will grow in the same soil as the other cyclamens, but the site should be a sheltered one, as it is slightly less hardy.

Cypripedium

The lady's slipper orchids are well worth the pampering they need

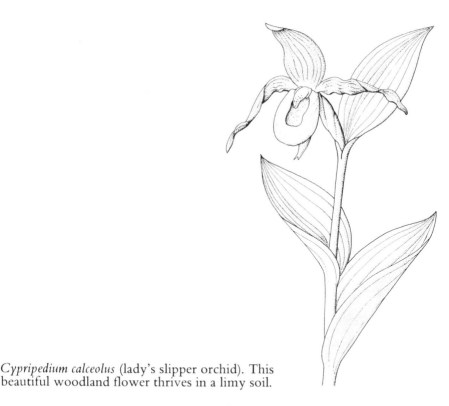

Cypripedium calceolus (lady's slipper orchid). This
beautiful woodland flower thrives in a limy soil.

to become established, for if they find themselves at home they will
thrive, and bestow an air of rare distinction.

C. calceolus: A rare British native that needs a limy soil—limestone grit or old mortar rubble should be mixed with peat and leaf
mould to make a planting compost. The fascinating flowers are
maroon and pale yellow, and the plant attains about 40 cm (16 in) in
height. Planting should be at a 25 cm (10 in) spacing.

C. reginae: An American ground orchid with strikingly beautiful white and rose-pink flowers, with lighter green leaves than
C. calceolus, and taller, reaching about 80 cm (32 in). Plants may be
spaced 40 cm (16 in) apart.

Digitalis purpurea

The foxglove; the British purple-flowered species is best for
naturalizing. The showy 'Excelsior' hybrids need constant replac-
ing, and look slightly out of place in the shade. The distinctive
shape of the flower spike held above the broadly pointed leaves
makes it an ideal foil for rounded, mound-forming plants. Foxgloves seed themselves very prolifically, and seeds should be sown
every year, whether *in situ* or not, because the plant is biennial.
New plants may be spaced about 30 cm (12 in) apart.

Digitalis purpurea (foxglove). An easily grown plant with handsome purple or white flowers.

Eranthis hyemalis (winter aconite), provides a touch of bright yellow in mid-winter.

Eranthis hyemalis

The winter aconite, flowering in January, has cheerful buttercup-yellow flowers which make a charming drift at the base of shrubs. Tubers may be planted about 15 cm (6 in) apart.

Erythronium dens-canis

The dog's-tooth violet, which is found wild in Britain, makes a charming mottled-green carpet, about 15 cm (6 in) high, with 5 cm (2 in) rosy-purple flowers appearing in March and April. It grows well in all types of soil, and is never happier than when naturalized in light woodland. There are pink and white-flowered varieties which are equally as good. The bulbs should be spaced about 10 cm (4 in) apart.

Ferns

The ferns have a special value in the woodland garden. The creeping, colonizing kinds take their place among the ground coverers, while the clump-forming species contrast dramatically in form with the broad-leafed evergreens in particular—the rhododendrons, for instance, or the camellias. A shady bank may be given over to ferns of both types in a mixture, for in this situation the many subtle variations in their greenness may be seen to advantage. Several of them, especially the broad-bladed hart's-tongue and the more typical clump-formers, have numerous named garden varieties, differing in the finely lobed division of their fronds. Some of these varieties are quite fantastically feathered, and it is always worth while, when buying ferns, to enquire if the nursery grows any of them.

Unlike flowering plants, ferns have two distinct generations in their life cycle. An examination of the undersides of fern fronds will often reveal dark brown bodies, or sporangia, which contain spores instead of true seeds, for the fern in its typical form is a sexless plant. As the sporangia ripen, the minute single-celled spores are ejected and carried far and wide on the breeze. Any one of these spores on germinating in moist soil is able to grow into an independent plant which few people would recognize as a fern: a scale-like structure barely 1 cm (less than $\frac{1}{2}$ in) long; yet this is a fern plant of the sexual generation. Called a prothallus, it bears the plant's reproductive organs. When rain or dew soaks the mature prothallus the external cells rupture, releasing microscopic sperms which make their way with the aid of lashing cilia through the film of moisture to seek the ovum in the tissue. A successful union results in a fern seedling of the familiar asexual generation. It develops attached to the prothallus until it is strong enough to strike roots and grow independently, by which time the prothallus itself has withered away.

There is, of course, no reason why fern spores should not be gathered and sown, simply scattering them over a moist, peaty surface; but success in germinating them will be unpredictable. Quite often, ferns grown beneath the staging in a glasshouse will seed themselves unattended—hart's-tongue is fond of doing this. Division is a standard way of propagating on a small scale in the case of the clump-formers, when a small piece can often be removed, and is used as a matter of course in the case of the spreading colonizers, when rooted portions can simply be lifted and replanted elsewhere. Where other methods are known, these are mentioned under the individual heads.

Clump-formers can be sited singly wherever they will be most effective, but the carpeting ferns should be planted at a spacing of about 15 cm (6 in).

Adiantum capillus-veneris: The maidenhair, a fern of strangely delicate appearance, often grown for florists' use. It likes mild, moist sites, where it colonizes slowly in shady crevices and among rocks. The fronds are deciduous and about 30 cm (12 in) long.

Adiantum pedatum: This species of maidenhair, with its distinctive, evenly shaped fronds, is much hardier than *capillus-veneris.*

Athyrium filix-femina: The lady fern, a worldwide plant of great beauty, it thrives in cool, moist sites where there is a loose, humus-rich or peaty soil. On such a site, in partial or full shade, it reaches its best development, with deciduous fronds up to 1 m (3 ft) long. On more open sites it grows strongly, but makes a shorter, stockier plant. The rootstock tends to grow out of the ground after a few seasons, and may occasionally need lifting and replanting.

Blechnum capense: A handsome evergreen with dark, 60 cm (24 in) long fronds, suitable for moist, sheltered situations in mild districts.

Blechnum penna-marina: An elegant 15 cm (6 in) high, dark green, carpet-forming fern, usually evergreen, suitable for moist, shady, sheltered sites and the tops of old walls.

Blechnum spicant: The hard fern, a common evergreen of northern countries, forming bright green tufts with fronds up to 90 cm (3 ft) long. It will not grow in limy soils, but prefers damp woodland banks in areas of acid soil where, if it feels at home, it will frequently seed itself.

Dryopteris dilatata: The broad buckler fern is one of the most widely distributed of northern ferns, occurring in hedgerows and shady places everywhere. It does not like lime and is not found naturally in limestone areas unless there is enough acid humus overlying the calcareous base to support it. It grows vigorously in moist, acid woods, where the fronds can reach 1·2 m (4 ft) in length.

Dryopteris filix-mas: The male fern, of similar size and appearance to the broad buckler, and almost as common in woods and hedges. The handsome fronds are arranged symmetrically around the clump like a giant shuttle-cock, and some sunshine is said to strengthen them, so that they last longer in the winter before withering. Apart from this, male fern is indifferent to its situation.

Gymnocarpium dryopteris: The oak fern, a deciduous, rapid colonizer of lime-free soil in moist, sheltered places, it has 23 cm (9 in) high fronds of an attractive, fresh green. The connection with oak is obscure, as it is by no means limited to oak woods. Found in many northern countries, it is rare in England but fairly common in the hills of Wales and Scotland.

Phyllitis scolopendrium: The hart's-tongue fern, also found in many northern countries, has smart, undivided fronds up to 60 cm (24 in) long. It enjoys a limy soil, but will manage anywhere—a slightly sloping site in shady woodland it finds ideal. Frequently it seeds itself freely, but if not, the hard, green, persistent frond bases

Phyllitis scolopendrium (hart's-tongue fern). This handsome evergreen enjoys the woodland shade.

may be removed after a leaf has withered, and potted up to produce new bulbils.

Polypodium vulgare: The polypody, a slow colonizer attaining 30 cm (12 in) in height, with close-growing, distinctive evergreen fronds. It enjoys a loose humus soil in shade, but will withstand dryness. A common plant worldwide, it often clothes walls and the stems and limbs of trees, and it thrives on limestone. It may be propagated by removing and replanting a portion of root with a growing tip.

Polystichum aculeatum: The hard shield, a handsome Old World fern, usually evergreen, the 60 cm (24 in) long fronds persisting over winter. It is a clump-former which enjoys a loose humus–rich soil and light shade, but in the wild it grows on steeper, rockier sites than the soft shield fern which it resembles.

Polystichum setiferum: The soft shield fern enjoys a woodland site. The elegant 60 cm (24 in) fronds on the slowly-spreading clumps are deciduous, falling in the autumn. It sometimes forms embryonic plants along the undersurface of its fronds, when these may be pegged down to allow them to root independently.

Thelypteris phegopteris: The beech fern, a plant with very dainty light green deciduous fronds about 23 cm (9 in) long. It will manage on limestone, but prefers a lime-free site. A slow colonizer, it has no obvious connection with beech woods, despite its name.

Galanthus

The snowdrops deserve to be planted in broad drifts. The common *G. nivalis* must be favourite for its dainty, fragile beauty—unless they are to be seen from a distance, in which case the large-flowered *G. elwesii* is perhaps preferable. There are several varieties which vary in their time of flowering, the size of their flowers, whether double or not, and in the green or yellow colouring at the petal tips. Plant 7·5 cm (3 in) apart.

Galax aphylla

Like a miniature evergreen lily of the valley, this little ground coverer loves a peaty woodland soil among shrubs, and is ideal for use beneath leggy rhododendrons. It may be planted at a 20–25 cm (8–10 in) spacing, and is propagated by dividing the creeping root-stock.

Helleborus

Pretty little plants for shady woodland sites where they can be well seen. Most of them may be divided after flowering, or seed may be sown as soon as it ripens. When conditions are good they may be sown *in situ*. Of outstanding value are: *H. atrorubens*, 30 cm (12 in) high, with purple-pink, green-centred flowers appearing in March and lasting until May; *H. foetidus*, an uncommon British plant which has deeply divided, dark evergreen leaves, and green, purple-stained flowers which appear during winter and early spring in large clusters: *H. niger*, the Christmas rose, 35 cm (14 in) tall, with pure white flowers from December to March; and *H. orientalis*, the Lenten rose, 45 cm (18 in) high, with flowers ranging from white through pink to crimson and purple, on display from January to March. For a drift, plant 23 cm (9 in) apart.

Hemerocallis

The day lily thrives in any lightly shaded, moist soil, and forms permanent though deciduous clumps which effectively buffer the more rampant spreaders. There are many splendid varieties, all of which may be planted at a 45 cm (18 in) spacing, and propagated by division in spring or autumn. Some of the most suitable are: 'Burning Daylight', 75 cm (30 in) tall, bright orange; 'Croesus', 75 cm (30 in) tall, gold; *H. dumortieri*, 60 cm (24 in) tall, very dense clumps, apricot; 'Hyperion', over 1 m (3 ft) tall, yellow; and *H. middendorffii*, 55 cm (22 in) tall, densely clumped, bright orange.

Helleborus orientalis (Lenten rose). White, pink, crimson or purple flowers are borne from January through to March.

These orange and yellow shades stand out best in the woodland garden, but there are some excellent crimson-flowered varieties also, such as 'Black Magic' and 'Stafford'.

Hosta

These wonderful contrast plants thrive in any reasonably moist soil, where they form steadily increasing weed-proof clumps of handsome foliage with lily-like flowers in the summer. They are deciduous, and die down completely in the winter when they may be difficult to locate, but appear early in the spring. Some of the best are: *H. crispula*, whose dark green leaves have a pure white border, and which should be planted at a 40 cm (16 in) spacing; *H. fortunei*, with broad, glaucous leaves and lilac flowers from July to September, to be planted 45 cm (18 in) apart; *H. glauca* 'Robusta', with immense, grey, rounded leaves, a marvellous plant with a bonus of lilac flowers on 1 m (3 ft) high stems in June and July, to be planted at 45 cm (18 in) spacing; *H. lancifolia*, with overlapping, narrow, pointed leaves and lilac flowers on 45 cm (18 in) stems, to be planted at 35 cm (14 in) spacing; *H. plantaginea* 'Grandiflora', with large, glossy green leaves and fragrant white flowers from August to October, to be planted 40 cm (16 in) apart; and *H. undulata* 'Erromena', with large, wavy, variegated leaves and dark lavender flowers from July to September, for a 50 cm (20 in) spacing. All may be propagated by division in winter or spring.

Lilium

The Martagon, Hanson and Pardalinum types of lily all lend themselves enthusiastically to naturalizing in the woodland garden. Many, especially the pale coloured ones such as the yellow-flowered *L. hansonii* tend to bleach in full sun. Often, the paler flowers are seen to best advantage against a dark background, and the two trumpet lilies, 'Green Dragon' and 'Mount Everest'—both outstanding white varieties only faintly flushed with colour—are excellent on the woodland edge. *L. martagon* itself, the Turk's cap lily, has purple flowers on 90 cm (3 ft) stems, and revels in the humus-rich woodland soil, though perhaps the flower colour does not show up quite so well. The scarlet Turk's cap, *L. chalcedonicum*, has a bright enough red to enable it to stand out dramatically, however shady the background, and it has the advantage of rarely exceeding 1 m (3 ft) in height. *L. martagon* 'Album' is the white Turk's cap, 1·2 m (4 ft) high, and can be really effective.

The Marhan hybrids are all strong-growing woodland lilies up to 1·8 m (6 ft) tall, ranging in colour from pale yellow through pink and buff to maroon red. The variety 'Mrs R. O. Backhouse' is a bright yellow, and 'J. S. Dijt' is basically cream, strongly speckled with orange and purple. There is a delicate, orchid-like quality about the multi-flowered lilies that has the effect of softening any harshness there might be in the colour. *L. pyrenaicum* 'Aureum' is the yellow Turk's cap, and one of the best for leaving to grow completely wild in the woodland glade.

Of the Pardalinums, *L. pardalinum* itself is the California lily, a strongly multi-flowered type—there may be as many as twenty individual flowers on each 1·5 m (5 ft) stem—and is a deep crimson-orange, while *L. pardalinum* 'Giganteum' is similar only much taller, the stems reaching nearly 2·5 m (8 ft).

The Bellingham hybrids are a mixed bag of 2 m (7 ft) tall woodland lovers, all multi-flowered, ranging in colour from yellow through orange to scarlet. The easily grown Shuksan lily of this type has the same deep, glowing orange hues on 1·2 m (4 ft) stems that show up best in moderate shade.

When lilies are being planted, they should be set about 10–15 cm (4–6 in) deep and partially covered with soil, then a good handful of rich compost or well-rotted cow manure should be added, before the final covering of soil. The first layer of soil is to keep the rich organic material from the newly emerging roots, so that it percolates gradually. A mulch of leaf mould or bracken should be given to prevent the soil drying out and, if possible, this good practice should be continued annually. It is also advisable to dead-head naturalized lilies to dissuade them from the weakening process of setting seed. For massing, they may be planted 40 cm (16 in) apart.

Maianthemum bifolium

A 15 cm (6 in) high mat former with fragrant lily of the valley flowers in the spring, useful for cool, moist places beneath shrubs. Propagation is by division of the creeping rootstock, and plants should be set 25 cm (10 in) apart.

Meconopsis

Beautiful 'poppies' which have great value both as dot plants and in small drifts, but one should be prepared to replace them should they disappear after flowering. The most perennial species are: *M. betonicifolia*, the blue poppy, flowering in May and June and attaining a height of 90 cm (3 ft); its variety 'Alba' with white flowers; *M. grandis* with deep blue flowers, 75 cm (30 in) high; and *M. villosa*, yellow-flowered in July, 60 cm (24 in) high. Propagation is by seed. For a drift, they should be planted 30 cm (12 in) apart.

Paeonia

The paeonies are useful clump formers, although their foliage is deciduous. They enjoy the richest soil available, and this may be acid or limy. Propagation is by division in the early autumn. There are numerous varieties, both single and double flowered, and some of the most striking are: 'Alba Plena', double white; 'Rosea Plena', double pink; 'Rubra Plena', double crimson—these three old-fashioned varieties all flowering in May and all about 60 cm (24 in) tall; 'Felix Crousse', bright crimson; 'Lady Alexandra Duff', scented pink; 'Sarah Bernhardt', pale pink; and 'Solange', pale apricot—some well-tried double varieties all flowering in June and growing about 75 cm (30 in) tall. For massing, they may be planted 40 cm (16 in) apart.

Primula

Most members of this huge and varied family love moisture, coolness and light shade. They are all propagated from seed sown either in the autumn or early spring, but sometimes the crown may be divided in the autumn. The British primrose *P. vulgaris* makes an ideal evergreen cover between shrubs, flowering typically in

March and April, but odd flowers may be seen all the year round. For naturalizing it should be planted at a 22 cm (9 in) spacing. Variety 'Wanda' is dwarf but vigorous, and of a striking vinous crimson. *P. juliae* is another dwarf primrose with deep lilac flowers, and it forms reliably dense mats of evergreen foliage. Planting should be at about a 15 cm (6 in) spacing for a good cover. *P. elatior* is the oxlip, a European plant rare in England, with slightly nodding sulphur-yellow flowers on 15 cm (6 in) stalks from March to May. It appreciates a moist, lightly shaded site, and should be set at a spacing of 23 cm (9 in). Bought seed under this name is usually of hybrid origin, and the many different colours which result are always very attractive, and not at all garish. *P. florindae*, a Tibetan species which needs a moist soil—it is quite happy growing actually in shallow water—bears 85 cm (34 in) high stalks with round clusters of yellow and orange flowers in June and July. The foliage is deciduous, but the clumps are thick enough to smother weeds, and plants may be set 35 cm (14 in) apart. *P. japonica* makes a wonderful drift of purplish red flowers on 45 cm (18 in) stalks in May and June, for moist, humus-rich soils at a 30 cm (12 in) spacing. Good varieties of *japonica* are 'Miller's Crimson' and 'Postford White'. Polyanthus are also excellent for naturalizing in their many hybrid strains. They should be planted 23 cm (9 in) apart, and will seed themselves if they like the site.

Scilla nutans

The bluebell. Who can imagine a spring woodland scene without at least a patch of blue carpet here and there? There are white and pink varieties to choose from, besides the old-fashioned blue. Bulbs should be planted 23 cm (9 in) apart.

A woodland plot

In the diagram opposite blue anemones and chionodoxas have been used freely throughout the area. All the plants listed grow equally well in acid or limy soil, with the exception of *Gaultheria procumbens*. In limy conditions, a good substitute for this would be *Sarcococca humilis*; another interesting choice would be *Tiarella cordifolia*. The more conservative gardeners might fall back on the infallible *Hypericum calycinum*, in which case a glance at the plan will suggest that the bergenias might be extended to meet the paeony clump, unless some other barrier plant is introduced, otherwise the hypericum is sure, sooner or later, to invade the *Oxalis oregana*.

The area, in effect, is a broad border, shaded fairly heavily and with rapidly increasing intensity from front to rear. Two small rock outcrops present a familiar problem. Rocks and dry walls are easy to clothe attractively when they are sited in full sunshine, but the list of plants suitable for these situations in the shade is a short one. *Omphalodes verna* can take the place of sun-lovers such as aubrieta in these circumstances, and a splash of bright colour can also be provided by *Acaena microphylla*. *Helxine soleirolii* is a natural

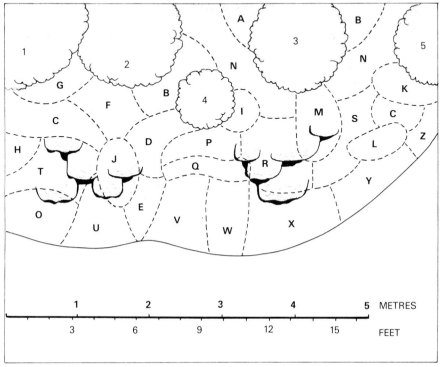

Detail from the front of a woodland plot demonstrating the use of dot plants.

Key
1 *Elaeagnus pungens* 'Maculata'
2 *Phillyrea decora*
3 *Aucuba japonica*
4 *Ruscus hypoglossum*
5 *Daphne pontica*

A *Acanthus spinosus*
B *Digitalis purpurea*
C *Hosta glauca* 'Robusta'
D *Hosta crispula*
E *Hosta lancifolia*
F *Asarum europaeum*
G *Polystichum setiferum*
H *Blechnum penna-marina*
I *Athyrium filix-femina*
J *Helleborus* varieties
K *Hemerocallis dumortieri*
L *Astilbe* 'Bressingham Beauty'
M *Paeonia* 'Rubra Plena'

N *Viburnum davidii*
O *Omphalodes verna*
P *Vancouveria hexandra*
Q *Vancouveria planipetala*
R *Acaena microphylla*
S *Gaultheria procumbens*
T *Helxine soleirolii*
U *Primula* 'Wanda'
V *Waldsteinia ternata*
W *Alchemilla alpina*
X *Oxalis oregana*
Y *Bergenia* 'Evening Light'
Z *Polygonum affine* 'Lowndes Variety'

for shady rocks—not showy, but always pleasing, it has something of that tranquil quality that Japanese gardens are supposed to convey.

Shady outcrops such as these may be accentuated by bordering clump-formers, planted as much for their own sake as to contain the vigorous scramblers such as the helxine. Paeonies—selected for appropriate height as well as flower colour; hellebores, which frequently seed themselves, allowed to spread down the edge of the rocks in a tumbling, scrambling colony; hostas, of a size, shape and leaf colour selected to match the adjoining under-storey carpeters; ferns—the colonizing types such as *Blechnum penna-marina* if there is room, or the clump-formers to give height. In this instance the soft shield fern works with the broad, grey leaves of *Hosta glauca* 'Robusta', making a sweeping curve with the hellebores to frame the rocks on the left of the diagram. The other outcrop is exaggerated by siting the tall, arching lady fern on the one side, and the low, thick clump of dark paeony on the other.

6
The Informal Hedge

Our carefully nurtured 'wild' woodland appearance will tend to lose some of its effect if it is presented against a background of severely trimmed formal hedge. Neatly clipped hawthorn, privet, beech, yew and holly are absolutely invaluable in their proper place—the formal garden, or the footpath boundary where there is no room to spare. But there are many alternatives which will do the job quite as well, while at the same time entering into the spirit of the woodland garden, and contributing to the general effect in terms of form, colour of foliage and flowering display.

For ornamental informality, those shrubs which constitute a hedge must be treated as shrubs and allowed, within reason, to adopt their own characteristic shape. In keeping with this, secateurs are called for rather than shears, not only to keep new growth within bounds, but always with a view to enhancing the following year's display.

Many ornamental hedging shrubs form quite as animal-proof a barrier as hawthorn—but even a hawthorn hedge can become gappy. The traditional farm hedge technique of laying and plashing the branches is not usually appropriate for the ornamental hedge. It can be done with the taller, more vigorous kinds but, often, it is better to run wire netting along the base of the plants, rather than to fret and fuss over leggy growth.

No less than when making a choice of under-storey plants, the height factor is all important, and the following list of suitable ornamental hedgers is graded according to their effective hedge-height, starting with the tallest:

Syringa
The lilacs really need plenty of room to act as a hedge, but they are unbeatable where a tall, flowering barrier is required. They respond well to winter manuring, or a mulch of compost annually. Propagate by layering, cutting a tongue through a bud node

HT

o ft)

HEIGHT   15–20 cm (6–8 in) from the tip of a strong shoot. Plant at 80 cm (32 in) spacing. Trimming should be carried out after flowering is

3 m (10 ft)   finished in the spring.

Viburnum tinus

A marvellous winter-flowering hedge for town, country or seaside, it carries its showy pinky-white flowers through till the spring. Evergreen except in the coldest areas, with bright red young bark. Plants may be layered, making a slight twist 15–20 cm (6–8 in) from the shoot tip and using a sandy compost. Planting is at a 45 cm (18 in) spacing. Trimming when necessary should be done in the spring.

Forsythia intermedia 'Spectabilis'

One of the loveliest of hedges, succeeding in polluted industrial areas. Make sure not to buy the floppy *F. suspensa* which is not suitable for use as a hedge. Cuttings may be taken during the summer and set in a shaded frame; alternatively, 20 cm (8 in) hardwood cuttings may be taken in the autumn and set out in open, sandy beds. Planting may be at a 50 cm (20 in) spacing. Trimming

2·8 m (9 ft)   should be limited to late spring after flowering is finished.

Viburnum tinus. An evergreen, winter-flowering shrub which makes a fine hedge.

HT
Viburnum opulus 'Sterile'

(9 ft)
The snowball bush, with huge balls of white flower in the spring, and attractive autumn tints before the leaves are shed. As a hedge, it is not keen on exhaust fumes from busy roads, but thrives in most situations. Young shoots may be layered during the summer, making a slight twist 15 cm (6 in) from the shoot tip. Planting is at a 70 cm (28 in) spacing. Trimming should be done as soon as flowering is finished in June.

Pyracantha

The firethorns give magnificent displays of berries, grow in any soil or situation, form a hedge quite as animal-proof as hawthorn, and have the advantage of being evergreen. Three of the best to use are: *P. angustifolia*, *P. coccinea* 'Lalandei', and *P. rogersiana*. Cuttings of 5–10 cm (2–4 in) side-shoots may be taken in August and kept shaded. Planting, using container-grown plants, should be at a 75 cm (30 in) spacing. Trimming should be given sparingly, and only when necessary to keep them in bounds, otherwise the effect produced by the arching shoots will be lost.

Ribes sanguineum

(8½ ft)
The flowering currant, very hardy and adaptable to any situation, makes a closely compact hedge which is a picture when in flower during the spring. 15 cm (6 in) cuttings may be taken at any time, either with a heel or at a node, and these will root outdoors in sandy beds. Planting should be at a 35–40 cm (14–16 in) spacing, and trimming should be carried out immediately after the flowers have finished.

Deutzia

All the many varieties of *Deutzia* will readily form a hedge in most situations, including town centres and the seaside. Very ornamental, with masses of pink or white flowers in midsummer. Cuttings may be taken at any time during the summer, either with a heel or at a node, and set in a shaded frame. Planting should be at a 75 cm (30 in) spacing. The wood that has flowered may be pruned out in the autumn, but the young shoots must be left untouched, or the following year's flowers will be lost.

Cotoneaster franchetii

A glossy evergreen hedger, covered with bees when the tiny white flowers are out in the spring, and with red berries to follow. It is not fussy regarding soil or situation. Propagation may be from seed, or
(8 ft)
by side-shoots taken with a heel in July, and set individually into

small pots, using a shaded frame. Planting should be at a 35 cm (14 in) spacing. Trimming is seldom needed except to keep the hedge within bounds.

Cotoneaster simonsii

A deciduous cotoneaster which can be kept clipped short as a formal hedge if desired. It always bears a good crop of bright red berries, and is usually grown from seed. Spacing should be at 35 cm (14 in), and trim as required to keep it within bounds.

Berberis stenophylla

A graceful, arching evergreen that becomes wreathed with golden flowers in April and May, and makes a wonderful, prickly, dog-proof hedge. Cuttings may be taken with a heel in October and November, and overwintered in a cold frame. Planting should be at a 35 cm (14 in) spacing. For the flowers to be seen at their best each year, trimming with secateurs should be carried out after flowering, allowing the young shoots to remain.

Rosa moyesii

One of the tallest rose hedgers, it is inclined to grow a little loosely in habit, so should be trimmed back quite hard each spring. It bears very showy single maroon flowers that are followed by bottle-shaped hips. Propagation may be by seed, otherwise 20–25 cm (8–10 in) cuttings may be taken in October or November, and set out in sandy beds. Planting should be at a 35–40 cm (14–16 in) spacing.

Cornus alba 'Sibirica'

The dogwood, with brilliantly scarlet twigs that give so valuable a splash of colour during the dull winter months. Variety 'Spaethii' has variegated leaves, and there is a bonus of pleasant autumn tints before the leaves fall. A hedge that does well in any soil or situation. Shoots may be layered in June or July, preferably giving them a slight twist at the point to be rooted. Planting is at a 50 cm (20 in) spacing. It may be trimmed hard in the spring to encourage twiggy young growth. The dogwoods are frequently constituents of old farm hedges, and they respond well to plashing and hard, annual trimming.

Philadelphus

The mock orange, in its several varieties, all bearing the well known sweetly scented flowers so prolifically, makes a marvellous hedge in any soil or situation. Cuttings of 10 cm (4 in) side-shoots

Philadelphus (mock orange). Bears sweetly scented white flowers in the spring.

(6½ ft) will root readily in a shaded frame. Planting should be at an 80 cm (32 in) spacing. Trimming should be carried out soon after flowering in the spring.

Buddleia davidii

The butterfly bush makes an unusual but effective hedge. There are numerous very showy varieties, their flower colours varying from white through lilac-pink to the deepest crimson-purple, but the fragrant mauve flowers of the semi-wild, naturalized form are most attractive to butterflies. Propagation is by tip-cuttings taken in the summer, and these root very readily in a shaded frame. Planting should be at a spacing of 70 cm (28 in). It should be cut back hard every year in March.

Olearia haastii

The daisy bush, quite hardy and accommodating except in very cold areas, happy at the seaside and in town centres. An evergreen with thick leathery leaves, and clusters of white daisy-like flowers in the summer. Side-shoots 5–10 cm (2–4 in) long may be taken with a heel during November, and set to overwinter in a cold frame. Spacing should be at 40 cm (16 in). Trimming may be

(6 ft)

HEIGHT   carried out in late winter or early spring, though the fluffy seed-heads may be trimmed lightly in the autumn, if desired.

1·8 m (6 ft)

Rosa rugosa

A formidably thorny hedge with large, single, purple flowers, though there are equally good double-flowered varieties, and large red hips that last well and are showy during the winter. A species that will thrive in any situation and, unlike most roses, it enjoys a light soil. It may be grown either from seed, or by 25 cm (10 in) cuttings taken in October or November and set out in open, sandy beds. Planting should be at a 45 cm (18 in) spacing. Trim either in late winter or early spring.

Berberis darwinii

An excellent, prickly, evergreen hedge which will trim narrow and tall if required, suitable for town, country or seaside. It may be grown from seed, otherwise 15 cm (6 in) cuttings with a heel may be taken in November and overwintered in a cold frame. Planting should be at a 35 cm (14 in) spacing. If grown as an informal hedge, trimming should be limited to the spring after the fine show of

1·6 m (5½ft)   orange flowers has finished.

Ceanothus thyrsiflorus

Pure blue flowers are rare, especially on hedges, and this species has large clusters of them in early summer. It needs a sheltered position in the country or by the seaside, is not too keen on town life, and prefers a light, well-drained soil. Cuttings of side-shoots with a heel should be taken in late spring, and set direct into small pots in a closed frame. Container-grown plants should be used, and spaced at 60 cm (24 in). An evergreen, this species requires very little trimming.

Rose Hybrids (Tall hedges)

'Queen Elizabeth', clear pink; 'Chinatown', yellow tinted pink, very fragrant; 'Nevada', pale creamy white; 'Fred Loads', orange-vermilion, very fragrant; 'Joseph's Coat', tricolor; 'Uncle Walter', scarlet and crimson; 'Golden Showers', yellow, very fragrant; 'Zéphirine Drouhin', bright carmine, fragrant. Roses will thrive in almost any soil, though they usually prefer the heavier kinds. Stable manure as a mulch is really beneficial to a rose hedge. 20–25 cm (8–10 in) cuttings may be taken during October or November and set outdoors in sandy beds. Spacing should be at

1·4 m (4½ft)   35–40 cm (14–16 in) in a well-prepared site. When first planted,

GHT

(4½ ft)

they should be cut back almost to ground level to encourage bushy growth to spring up from the base. A solid framework can be built up by judicious pruning, but any dead or weak growth should be cut right out. Once the hedge is well formed, a light trim in the winter or early spring is all that is required.

Spiraea menziesii 'Triumphans'

A very accommodating spiraea suitable for any site, originating in the western United States and thriving on dry soils provided they are not too alkaline. It becomes covered with bright, mauve-red flowers in August and, although leafless during the winter, the shoots have a rich brown colour. Plants will sometimes divide, otherwise cuttings may be taken during December and rooted in open, sandy beds. Plant at a 60 cm (24 in) spacing, and trim hard during early spring.

Escallonia

1 (4½ ft)

Many of the species and varieties make very attractive evergreen hedges with masses of red, pink or white flowers in summer or autumn, varying from variety to variety. Two of the hardiest and best for hedging are *E. langleyensis* with bright cherry pink flowers, and 'Crimson Spire' with bright crimson flowers. They are not fussy regarding soil type, and are excellent for use by the seaside where they will withstand salt spray. In mild areas, 15–20 cm (6–8 in) cuttings with a heel may be taken in November and set outdoors in sheltered beds. In other areas, smaller cuttings must be taken in July, using heeled side-shoots, and rooted in a closed frame. Planting should be at a 35 cm (14 in) spacing. They may be kept formally clipped if so desired, but for informal use they should be trimmed lightly after flowering. In the case of autumn-flowering kinds, trimming should be delayed until March.

Weigela 'Abel Carrière'

Grows very well in any situation or soil, with distinctively arching branches and bright carmine-pink flowers in May and June. Soft tip cuttings may be taken in July and rooted in a shaded frame, otherwise larger, harder cuttings with a heel may be taken in December, and set in sandy beds outdoors. Planting should be at an 85 cm (34 in) spacing. Trimming may be carried out after flowering is finished in June.

Hydrangea arborescens 'Grandiflora'

n (4 ft)

The large bunches of greenish flowers produced from July to September make this hedge a remarkable sight when growing on

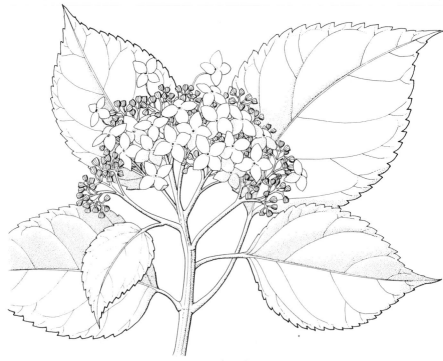

Hydrangea arborescens. Produces large bunches of greenish flowers from July to September.

1·2 m (4 ft)
the woodland edge. It does well in most soils. Cuttings of shoot tips 10 cm (4 in) long may be taken in July and set in a heated frame. Alternatively, propagation may be achieved by layering, when a convenient branch is pegged down in the spring and soil is simply mounded up around the new shoots. Planting should be at a 75 cm (30 in) spacing. Trim in late winter or early spring.

Hydrangea paniculata 'Grandiflora'

Another splendid hedging hydrangea which chances to have the same varietal name. The huge flowers it produces in summer and autumn are white, tinged with pink. Cuttings of 10 cm (4 in) tips may be taken in July at a node, choosing sturdy shoots for the purpose, and set in a shaded frame. Planting should be at a 75 cm (30 in) spacing. Trim in late winter or early spring.

Cydonia japonica

Japanese quince will grow in almost any soil, town or country, in sun or shade. The crimson flowers start to open in February. It may be grown from seed, otherwise layering may be carried out in the early spring, giving a slight twist to the shoot about 15 cm (6 in) from the tip. Space at 45 cm (18 in) apart. Trim back fairly hard

1·1 m (3½ ft)
after flowering to keep it in shape.

Rosa 'Penzance Briars'

Raised by crossing the sweet briar with the hybrid perpetuals, all the roses of this strain make really excellent hedges for any soil or situation. They are noted for their scented foliage, and flower colour varies with the variety. 20–25 cm (8–10 in) cuttings may be taken in the autumn and rooted in open, sandy beds. Planting should be at a 45 cm (18 in) spacing. Trim as necessary in early spring.

Weigela 'Eva Rathke'

This variety will grow anywhere in any soil, and is well known for its crimson trumpet-shaped flowers. It is more compact of growth than most of its genus. Propagation may be achieved with cuttings of soft tips taken in July and set in a shaded frame, or with harder 20 cm (8 in) cuttings taken in December and rooted overwinter in open, sandy beds. Spacing should be at 60 cm (24 in) intervals, and trimming may be carried out after flowering in the spring or early summer.

Rose Hybrids (Low hedges)

'Iceberg', pure white, tinged with pink in the bud; 'Peace', light yellow, edged with pink; 'Frensham', deep scarlet-crimson, very vigorous; 'Dorothy Wheatcroft', bright red; 'Super Star', very fragrant, vermilion; 'Scarlet Queen Elizabeth', scarlet, less vigorous than the pink 'Queen Elizabeth'; 'Masquerade', yellow, pink and red. These and all hybrid roses are normally propagated by budding onto stocks, thus ensuring a uniform standard of vigour but, as with the varieties listed for use as tall hedgers, 20 to 25 cm (8–10 in) cuttings taken in November and set out in sandy beds will root fairly readily, and the resultant plants will, of course, be free of suckers. Hedge spacing should be 35 cm (14 in). An annual mulch of stable manure is the best maintenance treatment. After planting they should be cut back to within 5 cm (2 in) of the ground to encourage them to bush out from the base, and annual trimming should be carried out in early spring.

Hypericum patulum 'Henryi'

An attractive hedge, bright with yellow flowers throughout the summer, growing well in any soil whether in sun or shade. Cuttings may be taken in July, using 10 cm (4 in) side-shoots with a heel, and set in a shaded frame. Alternatively, longer and harder cuttings may be taken in November and overwintered in a cold frame. Planting should be at a 40 cm (16 in) spacing. Trim if needed in early spring before the flower buds are formed.

HEIGHT

Spiraea thunbergii

0·9 m (3 ft)

A very hardy spiraea that grows well in any situation. It may be clipped as a formal hedge, but the attractive arching branches covered with white flowers in the spring are seen at their best in informal style. Plants may often be divided in the early spring, otherwise 10 cm (4 in) cuttings may be taken in June or July and set in a shaded frame, preferably using small, individual pots. Spacing should be at 45 cm (18 in), and trimming if necessary should be carried out after flowering is finished.

Fuchsia magellanica 'Riccartonii'

A lovely small hedge, covered during the summer with red and purple flowers. Occasionally, heavy frosts may kill the top growth, but it will shoot again from the base. Soft tip cuttings taken at a node in May or June will root very readily in a shaded frame. Planting should be at a 40 cm (16 in) spacing. Trimming should be limited to early spring.

Berberis thunbergii 'Atropurpurea'

0·8 m (2½ ft)

A very attractive, prickly little hedge with reddish-purple foliage. It will grow from 10 cm (4 in) cuttings with a heel, taken in the autumn and set in a cold frame. Planting should be at a 30 cm (12 in) spacing. It can be trimmed as a formal hedge if required, otherwise very light trimming only is necessary, and this should be done in the spring.

Potentilla fruticosa

There are many varieties of shrubby potentilla that will grow upright and compact so as to make excellent low hedges. It has one of the longest flowering seasons of any shrub, the primrose-yellow flowers covering the bushes throughout the summer. Short side-shoot or tip cuttings may be taken in July and kept well shaded, or similar but harder cuttings can be taken in the autumn and set in a cold frame. Propagating success varies from year to year—sometimes one hundred per cent rooting can be achieved. Hedge spacing should be 30 cm (12 in). The hedge should be trimmed only once annually, very lightly in the early spring.

Rosmarinus officinalis

Rosemary makes a very pretty and unusual hedge, but it prefers a warm, sunny site. 15 cm (6 in) cuttings with a heel taken in September will root readily under glass. Planting should be at a 45 cm (18 in) spacing. Rosemary will die back if cut too hard, so

0·7 m (2 ft)

trimming in early spring should be very light.

126

Potentilla fruticosa. Primrose-yellow
flowers are borne throughout the
summer.

Rosa spinosissima

1 (2 ft) The Scotch briars, in several varieties, all make really excellent,
fiercely-thorned hedges suitable for dry, light soils. There are
single and double flowered types, with yellow, white, pink or red
flowers. 'Altaica', with white flowers, is the most vigorous hedger.
Suckers may be removed for replanting, or 20 cm (8 in) cuttings
may be taken in October and set out in open, sandy ground.
Planting should be at a 37 cm (15 in) spacing, and light trimming
only is needed, in the spring.

Berberis wilsoniae

A prickly hedge with showy coral-red berries and brilliant autumn
foliage tints, growing well on exposed sites or by the seaside. It
may be grown from seed, otherwise 15 cm (6 in) cuttings with a
heel may be taken in October and set in a cold frame. Planting
should be at a 30 cm (12 in) spacing. Trim in the spring.

Cotoneaster microphylla

An excellent dwarf evergreen hedge, with small glossy green
leaves and red berries. 5–10 cm (2–4 in) cuttings with a heel may be
taken in July and rooted in a shaded frame. Planting should be at a
1 (2 ft) 30 cm (12 in) spacing. If necessary, trim lightly to retain shape.

127

Berberis wilsoniae. A prickly hedge bearing red berries and brilliantly coloured in autumn.

Hypericum × moserianum

0·6 m (2 ft)   An extremely accommodating low hedge for sun or shade, in moist or dry soils, well covered with yellow flowers during late summer. 10 cm (4 in) side-shoot cuttings with a heel may be taken during July and set in a shaded frame. Planting should be at a 25 cm (10 in) spacing, and trimming may be done either during late winter or early spring.

Spiraea japonica 'Anthony Waterer'

One of the best dwarf hedgers, covered with broad, flat heads of crimson flowers from July to October. There are variegated forms which are very attractive, but they are not as vigorous as the green-leaved type. New plants can sometimes be obtained by division, otherwise 10 cm (4 in) cuttings may be taken in December and set out in open, sandy beds. Planting should be at a 40 cm (16 in) spacing, and trimming, if required, is best done in early

0·5 m (1½ ft)   spring.

128

HT

(1½ ft)

Hebe 'Autumn Glory'

An evergreen, shrubby veronica with dark green leaves on reddish-brown shoots, covered with rich purple flower spikes from July to October. It does well at the seaside, and is not affected by industrial pollution, but, although hardier than most of its genus, 'Autumn Glory' is seen at its best in mild districts. 10 cm (4 in) cuttings may be taken at a node during June or July, and set under glass in a sandy compost. Planting should be at a 30 cm (12 in) spacing. Trim lightly, in late winter or early spring.

7

Plant Ailments

The autumn colours we admire so much appear at the end of the growing season, while the nutrients within the leaf tissue are being assimilated by the tree. Technically, therefore, such leaves are exhibiting symptoms of nutrient deficiency, and it follows that if similar colours appear during the summer, they are clear warning signs that should be heeded.

Insect damage also tends to follow specific patterns, and occasionally tree-killer diseases may strike with very little warning. It is as well to notice the health of one's plants, without necessarily indulging in some kind of floral hypochondria, for often the remedy is swift and simple, and can bring about a dramatic improvement in plant health.

Abnormalities of the leaves

Neat circular holes: Weevils.

They damage many kinds of plants, especially rhododendrons, and usually feed at night, but during the day they shelter at ground level under any cover they can find. Pieces of wood, pots, etc., placed on the ground will attract them, when they may be caught.

Neat rounded chunks, from the margin inwards: Leaf-cutting bees.

They do little damage, and there is no need for control.

Leaves distorted, spotted, scratched, with brown blotches developing into small holes: Capsid bugs.

Spray with systemic insecticide.

Ragged, erratic holes: Caterpillars.

Spray with contact or systemic insecticide.

Winding, discoloured trails: Leaf miners.

Spray with systemic insecticide and pick off infected leaves.

Leaves skeletonized: Tiny caterpillars.
Spray with insecticide.

Leaves white-marbled on upper surface: Leaf-hoppers.
Spray with systemic insecticide.

Rhododendron leaves white-marbled above, stained brown underneath: Rhododendron lace bugs.
Spray with systemic insecticide.

Leaves twisted and rolled: Sawfly and tortrix moth.
Spray with systemic insecticide or pick off infected leaves. On large trees such as the stalked oak there may be heavy infestation, for example by the oak tortrix moth, but there is little one can do on such a scale, and the tree normally recovers.

Brown ragged edges: Weather.
On large-leafed trees such as the horse chestnut this condition sometimes occurs during the summer following cold, drying winds early in the season. Similar damage can also be caused by an irregular water supply to the roots of large trees, and this is a difficult matter to put right.

Thickening and distortion of the leaf, in trees such as elm: Gall-mites.
Spray with systemic and contact insecticide in the spring.

Thickening and distortion of the leaf, in shrubs such as rhododendron: Frost damage in the bud.
There is nothing that can be done.

Thickening and distortion of the leaf, in Prunus *species—especially flowering almond:* Peach-leaf curl.
Spray with Bordeaux mixture before the flower buds open, and remove and burn infected leaves.

Leaves covered with black, sticky exudation: Sucking insects.
This is a secondary fungus growth on the honeydew exuded by the insects. Spray with insecticides.

Leaves powdered white: Mildew.
On shrubs, especially roses, spray with systemic fungicide or proprietary mildew sprays. On oak, small specimens may be sprayed, but large trees should come to no harm.

Black blotches: Fungal infection.
Rose black-spot is well known, and may be sprayed with one of the proprietary rose sprays. On sycamore and maples, black spots are caused by a different fungus. Trees usually come to no harm, but they may be sprayed with systemic fungicide if they

are small enough, and the infected leaves raked up and burnt.

Purple blotches, especially on leathery leaves such as rhododendron: Magnesium deficiency.
> Spray after flowering with magnesium sulphate or a proprietary foliar feed. 'Tonk's Formula' rose fertilizer and several brands of slow-acting general fertilizers also contain magnesium.

Rusty-coloured sticky stain on leaves: Rust fungus.
> There are sometimes tiny insects present in the rust, but these are only feeding on the fungus. The birches are often attacked. Spray with systemic fungicide.

Yellowing along the edges, old leaves dying: Potassium deficiency.
> Apply sulphate of potash at the rate of a small handful per square metre, and spray with a foliar feed.

Yellowing along the edges, spreading between the veins: Magnesium or manganese deficiency.
> Apply a fertilizer which contains trace elements, and spray with foliar feed.

Yellowing between the veins, becoming dead patches: Magnesium deficiency.
> Apply magnesium sulphate in the spring, a small handful per square metre, and spray with foliar feed.

Yellowing between the veins, with reduced leaf size: Zinc deficiency.
> Spray with foliar feed containing trace elements.

Yellowing along the veins: Oxygen starvation; water-logging.
> Discover the cause at the roots. Sometimes gas main leaks can do this.

General yellowing: Lime-induced chlorosis.
> Suffered by calcifugous plants growing in alkaline soils. On a small scale, treat with sequestered iron solution. On a larger scale, apply aluminium sulphate at the rate of a small handful per square metre, spray with a foliar feed, and mulch with peat.

Leaves small and pale, with red and yellow tints: Nitrogen deficiency.
> Apply ammonium sulphate, a very small handful per square metre, and also treat with a general slow-acting fertilizer.

Leaves with an overall purple coloration: Phosphate deficiency.
> Apply superphosphate of lime at the rate of a generous handful per square metre, and also treat with a general slow-acting fertilizer.

Leaves generally small and weak: General nutrient deficiency.
Regular mulching with manure or rich compost will avoid this.
General fertilizers and foliar feeds may also be used.

Abnormalities of buds and shoots

Buds badly deformed and scarred: Capsid bugs.
Spray with systemic insecticide.

Death of growing tips: General trace element deficiency.
Spray with foliar feed containing trace elements.

Death of growing tips, and thickening of leaf tissue: Boron deficiency.
Spray with foliar feed containing trace elements.

Buds soft and rotten: Frost damage.
Nothing can be done to save the affected buds, but attention should be given to avoiding frost-hollow formation. Cold air, like water, flows downhill, following the line of least resistance, and frost damage can often be avoided by ensuring an unimpeded flow—even to the extent, for instance, of leaving a gap at the lowest point of a hedge or wall.

Rhododendron flower buds dark brown and dead, bearing black, bristle-like structures: Rhododendron bud-blast.
This fungal disease is carried by an insect—the rhododendron leaf-hopper, a green bug with two red stripes. Spray with systemic fungicide to counter the fungus, and insecticide to kill the insect.

Abnormalities of bark and twigs

Bright red spots on the twigs: Coral-spot fungus.
On many small trees this fungus feeds saprophytically on wood that is already dead, but it may sometimes kill branches, especially on horse chestnut, European sycamore and lime. As a rule, the affected branches are those that should have been removed during cleaning operations.

Tiny red spots developing into a sunken black wound: Nectria canker.
Appearing in the spring on the bark of broadleafed trees, this is one of those fungi that are able to enter untreated wounds in the bark. If a canker develops, it must be treated as a cavity.

On sweet chestnut; yellow or orange spots on the bark: Chestnut blight.
The bark is killed, and in severe attacks the tree may be girdled so that the top dies. Infected trees will probably have to be removed.

On beech; small black lumps on the bark: Beech–bark disease.
A patch of bark dies and the disease spreads, eventually killing the tree. The infection is spread by aphis–like coccus insects that feed on the bark, and these should be searched for on the bark of healthy trees. Paraffin and a scrubbing brush are useful weapons.

On European sycamore; a black, sooty mass of spores on the bark: Sooty–bark disease.
The affected bark dies and the infection spreads, eventually killing the tree. There is no effective remedy.

Substantial fungi of various shapes, sizes and colours, appearing on the stems or roots: Bracket fungi.
These fungi sometimes lead to the formation of cavities, and eventually to hollow or dead trees. The dead tissue should be cut out and the wound treated as described in Chapter 3.

Sudden withering of the foliage

The direct cause of this is a disruption of the normal flow of sap or water, but there is usually a fungal disease responsible. In the case of very small or newly transplanted trees such a symptom may be due to lack of water, possibly caused by the interference of some creature—for instance, ants may have excavated around the roots.

Dutch elm disease
In effect, the leaves of an infected tree are dying of thirst, because the fungus responsible has blocked the cells which carry water from the roots. Another symptom appears in the small twigs among the upper crown: they tend to develop a characteristic bend like a shepherd's crook, and if such a twig is cut through, brown marks may be seen in a ring pattern. Many people have given up in the struggle against Dutch elm disease, but if the intention is to continue combating it, the following points should be taken into account:

1 Elm beetle larvae feed beneath the bark on weakened elms. If loose pieces of bark are removed, their characteristic feeding galleries may be seen.
2 The newly hatched adult beetles emerge from the bark at any time between May and October, depending on the weather, and fly away carrying spores of the fungus.
3 They alight usually high up among the crowns of elm trees, where they begin to feed on the tender bark in the crotches of twigs and the smaller branches. From this point of infection, the spores of the fungus spread down the branch within the current year's annual ring.

4 Although the disease can only spread slowly down through the wood, when it reaches a fork in the branches, the spores are carried rapidly up the new branch in the sap stream.
5 When the beetles are ready to breed they fly down to seek a patch of bark on a weakened elm tree, where they lay their eggs and the cycle starts again. If the winter is very cold, their numbers are reduced.

With this life cycle in mind, any attack on the disease must be three-pronged. It will be necessary to:

a) control the beetles;
b) combat the fungus;
c) strengthen the tree.

Once the sap can no longer flow along a branch, there is nothing that can be done to revive it; dead branches must be removed and burnt, otherwise the beetles will simply be provided with fresh breeding grounds. If possible, the crowns should be sprayed with both contact and systemic insecticides to kill the beetles. A systemic fungicide should be sprayed on the foliage and watered into the root feeding area, to attack the fungus. A foliar feed should also be applied in the same way, and the root feeding area must be dressed with a general fertilizer, to strengthen the tree.

Honey fungus

This fungus grows beneath the bark, and has the effect of blocking the flow of sap. It is quite as devastating on large forest trees as it is on small shrubs, and even herbaceous plants and bulbs may be attacked. Signs of infection may not appear for a full season. Sometimes infected plants fail to flower properly, but usually the first symptom of an attack is a wilting of part or all of the crown foliage. In the case of leathery-leafed plants like Portuguese laurel, it may show as a silvering of the foliage as the leaf tissues dry up and separate. The fungus spreads from tree to tree by means of black, bootlace-like growths or rhizomorphs which are able to travel for many metres beneath the surface of the soil and attach themselves to the tips of healthy tree roots, spreading from there under the bark to the stem. These rhizomorphs constitute proof of identification, but a quick check for infection can be made by scratching away a little soil from the base of the stem and removing a small piece of bark with a penknife. On infected trees, a white, fan-like fungal growth can be clearly seen spreading over the cambium, and this has a mushroomy smell. There are other fungi which cause so-called collar rot, but these lack the distinctive smell.

After a tree has been killed, honey-coloured toadstools sometimes appear at the base of the tree and on the roots, and spores given off from these may also infect other plants. Honey fungus is the usual cause of progressive dying in privet hedges, in which case the disease creeps along the hedgerow at the rate of a metre or two each year. Other trees and shrubs particularly prone to infection are: the birches; the cedars; *Chaenomeles*; cotoneasters; forsythias; hydrangeas; laburnums; lilacs; *Malus*—both domestic and crab apples; the Scots and Corsican pines; *Prunus*, all species and varieties, including flowering cherries; rhododendrons; roses; Sitka spruce; *Tsuga heterophylla*; viburnums and willows.

A phenolic compound known as 'Bray's emulsion' has been formulated specifically to deal with honey fungus. Treatment involves sterilizing the infected area by digging out the top-soil around the stem, exposing as much as possible of the root system, watering with the diluted emulsion, and saturating the top-soil with it as it is being replaced. In the case of large trees, holes may be bored through the bark, and some of the liquid injected into the cambium area.

8
Planting for all Seasons

There need be no dull season in the woodland garden. While winter still retains a grip, the hybrid almond 'Pollardii' will be flowering spectacularly, its deep pink blossoms standing out against a dark background of evergreen shade. In a sheltered spot the earliest camellia flowers add to the promise of spring, while the air is still faintly fragrant with vanilla from the winter heliotrope *Petasites fragrans*.

If *Hypericum calycinum* has been used to the forefront of the wood, it can be clipped hard back in February or early March so as to thicken it into an even, compact carpet. This treatment will also allow chionodoxa bulbs to be introduced to wonderful effect, for their intensely sky-blue flowers will clothe the area before the new hypericum leaves start to grow. Daffodils may also be planted amongst them in the same way, but daffodil leaves tend to persist a little too thickly and, if cutting back is done, it must be finished in good time so as not to decapitate the daffodils, for they will start to shoot all the earlier for being snug amidst the rose of Sharon.

The blue anemones *A. apennina* and *A. blanda*, together with the dog's-tooth violet *Erythronium dens-canis*, also make a colourful show at this time, anticipating the bluebells which will follow in the late spring, so that all the blue carpeting is over and done with before the main woodland canopy takes full leaf.

The magnificent pink flowers of *Magnolia campbellii* and the pure white, fragrant ones of *M. denudata* will be fully open before mid-March. Among the rhododendrons the rosy-purple 'Praecox' by this time will virtually have finished flowering, only to be followed in succession by 'Cilpinense' of palest pink, the dark pink of 'Tessa', and the bright yellow 'Valaspis'. Then there will be the deep, glowing crimson of the species rhododendron, *R. barbatum*, followed by another crimson—the tree rhododendron 'Cornubia'. In late spring when the bulk of rhododendrons and azaleas come into flower, the woodland garden scene is unforgettable—but this

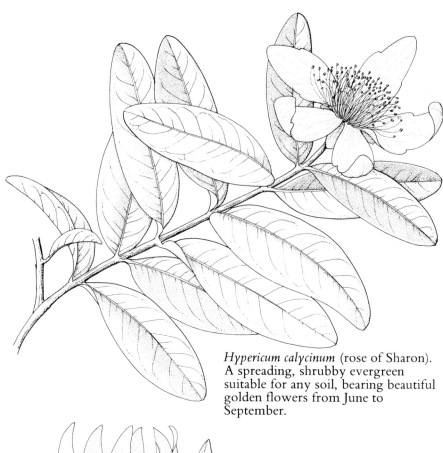

Hypericum calycinum (rose of Sharon).
A spreading, shrubby evergreen
suitable for any soil, bearing beautiful
golden flowers from June to
September.

Erythronium dens-canis (dog's
tooth violet). Spreads to form a
charming carpet, with purple
flowers in the spring.

is only possible with an acid soil, for rhododendrons stubbornly refuse to grow if any lime is present.

The choice of shrubs which will tolerate lime is still wide, but flower colours tend to be paler, with the pure white of the several philadelphus varieties, the pink and white of the deutzias, the pastel yellow shades of all the mahonias and, later in the season, the blue of *Hydrangea villosa*—one of the few hydrangeas to keep its blue colour well under alkaline conditions—all excellent tones to set against a dark background. Patches of brilliance can be introduced by using the Turk's-cap lilies as dot plants or in clumps, in the partial shade around the taller shrubs.

Leaf colour should be used to the full throughout the growing season—not forgetting the variegated evergreens such as *Elaeagnus pungens* 'Maculata'. Many of the best trees for autumn colour, such as the maples, are also highly ornamental both during the growing season and in the winter, with their handsome striated bark. But one can scarcely spare the space to plant purely for autumn leaf colour—some compromise has to be made. A good purple-leafed tree is *Cotinus coggygria* 'Royal Purple', a splendid dark foil for yellow foliaged trees such as *Robinia pseudoacacia* 'Frisia', a planting combination that shows them both to great advantage. The cotinus can be kept trained or clipped as a bush or as ground cover, a role it fills quite willingly, and in this form it blends most beautifully with the soft yellow flowers of the potentillas. Another effective combination of purple and yellow can be obtained by planting the hazel *Corylus avellana* 'Aurea' in front of the filbert *C. maxima* 'Purpurea', and both these plants may be grown either as standard trees or multi-stemmed shrubs. The best yellow-leafed tree of all, perhaps, is *Catalpa bignonioides* 'Aurea' which, however, prefers full sun and needs a great deal of room to develop fully.

For a charming combination nearer the ground on the woodland edge, there is the blue Tibetan poppy, *Meconopsis betonicifolia*, planted in association with the crimson candelabrum *Primula japonica*, particularly right for peaty soil, for the blue poppy will not colour well when lime is present. Primulas are easy to match and, indeed, a drift of primulas of any colour will look right in almost any combination.

Splendid contrasts in shape and form may be achieved by using the ferns and the hostas. Hostas look particularly good with the later flowering azaleas, which otherwise might tend to be too brilliant, even gaudy. The sculptured greens and blue-greys of the hostas tone them down and link them charmingly with the other less colourful woodlanders. Ferns of the frond-making type are excellent in association with rhododendrons, especially the broader leafed kinds. It is just this mellow contrast in form that makes the woodland garden a place of such fascination at all seasons. Hostas, of course, die back for the winter, and it is difficult then to find them if they need moving, but fortunately they always seem to transplant just as successfully if moved around while still in leaf.

In midsummer, the last of the rhododendrons—the late flowerers such as the blood-red 'Arthur Lisborne' and 'Rubina'—will be contrasting boldly with the showy white flower bracts of the tree dogwoods, *Cornus controversa*, *C. kousa* and *C. nuttallii*, while the eucryphias and hydrangeas carry the flowering season well into autumn.

The white stems of the birches make a good background for any plant, and they themselves stand out to perfection against the black-green of yew, rhododendron, and Portuguese laurel. As they lose their leaves, the birches will allow the free autumn flowering of cyclamen massed at their roots, the clumps spreading a little each year. All the small bulbs and little woodland plants, the wood sorrel and the anemones, thrive under birches, and, frequently, the larger, shade-bearing shrubs are able to find their ideal environment under such a lightly foliaged canopy.

During the coldest months, the witch hazel and the winter-flowering jasmine are not the only flowers to be seen, neither is yellow the only winter flower colour available, for *Viburnum tinus* is covered the winter through with its waxy, pinkish-white sprays, and the white *Sarcococca* fills the air with fragrance from Christmas on.

Many plants as purchased from the nursery are container-grown, or at least containerized, and these can be planted at any time, so every advantage can be taken of the seasons. It is difficult sometimes to assess just how shady a particular spot will be if it is examined only in midwinter or early spring. Crowns can be lightened during high summer, as we have seen, and the use of containerized plants means that new plantings can take place as and when they are seen to be desirable.

A basic planting scheme for a small plot
Using the principles outlined, this scheme will produce the nearest approach possible to an ornamental woodland within the confines of an average sized plot, for enjoyment at all seasons, without limiting the choice of trees to the dwarf kinds, or risking domination by a few kinds more vigorous than the rest.

Planting is in three phases, which may be completed either simultaneously, or there may be a lapse of several seasons between each, while the tree canopy is developing. In the latter case, the garden can still be used for other purposes—for flowers, vegetables or lawn—after the first phase has been completed.

The main background trees are a solitary *Acer lobelii* and a group of three silver birch, these forming a framework to the main planting, and themselves backed by the dark, contrasting foliage of *Prunus lusitanica* and the taller-growing rhododendrons if the soil is an acid one. *Acer lobelii* may exceed 15 m (49 ft) in height, but its distinctively columnar habit will keep it within bounds. Other maples included in the scheme are *A. griseum, A. davidii* and *A. palmatum*, the last named grown as a small, wide-spreading shrub. From the main house viewpoint, which is taken to be the bottom, central area on the diagram, a good display has been planned for each season. During the spring, one's attention will inevitably be captured by the closely-planted group of flowering cherries near the house. Centrally among them is 'Kanzan', with its stiffly ascending branches smothered in heavily double, deep pink blossom—mellowed by the paler semi-double pink of the upright 'Amanogawa' to the front. Bounding this, and in strong contrast, is the graceful 'Cheal's Weeping Cherry', or the closely similar 'Kiku-shidare Sakura', brushing the ground with its double pink blooms. Behind this trio, the wide-spreading 'Jo-nioi', often said to be the most beautiful of the single white flowered cherries, and so very effective in offsetting any feeling of excess that such a wealth of pink blossom might bring. The group is balanced by a single specimen of *Prunus cerasifera* 'Nigra', also in bloom at this time, its petals delicately pink against the richly purple twigs.

To the forefront of this self-contained grove of spring-flowering trees, and surrounding the dark evergreen camellias—themselves still in full flower during cherry blossom time—are the primulas, primroses and polyanthus, which may be allowed to seed themselves and run riot in a random mixture of colour.

Looking to the left from the same viewpoint, if chionodoxa has been planted among the rose of Sharon—and the hypericum will have been cut back a few weeks earlier—the clustered flowers will be forming an eye-catching carpet of blue. Quite a few dozen bulbs will be needed to allow them to rampage freely around the stems of the two spring-flowering magnolias. The nearest of these, *Magnolia stellata*, opens in March and continues opening new flowers throughout April. There is always the danger that these early magnolia flowers will get nipped by frost and spoiled, but *M. stellata* produces them in such profusion, and over so prolonged a succession, that one would have to be particularly unlucky to lose them all. Behind this, the taller *M. soulangiana* has huge

0   3   6   9   12   METRES

0   6   12   18   24   30   36   42   FEET

A basic planting scheme for a small plot

First Phase: FOR ACID OR LIMY SOILS

A *Acer lobelii*
B *Betula pendula*
C *Acer griseum*
D *Arbutus unedo*
E *Salix* 'Chermesina' pollarded at 1·5 m (5 ft)
F *Salix* 'Chermesina' pollarded at ground level
G *Salix* 'Vitellina' pollarded at ground level
H *Acer davidii*
I *Cornus controversa*
J *Sorbus sargentiana*
K *Amelanchier asiatica*
L *Sorbus* 'Joseph Rock'
M *Magnolia soulangiana*
N *Magnolia stellata*
O *Prunus* 'Jo-nioi'
P *Prunus cerasifera* 'Nigra'
Q *Prunus* 'Cheal's Weeping Cherry'
R *Prunus* 'Kanzan'
S *Prunus* 'Amanogawa'

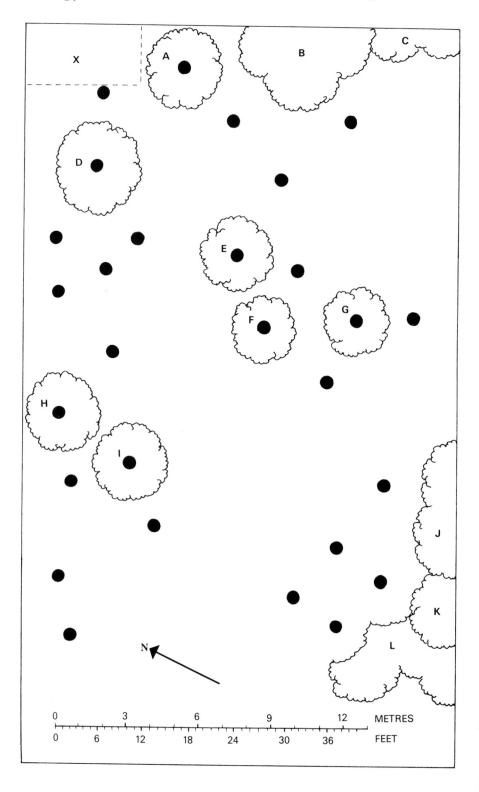

A basic planting scheme for a small plot—continued

Second Phase: FOR ACID SOILS

A *Prunus lusitanica*
B *Rhododendron* taller varieties
C *Buddleia davidii*
D *Styrax japonica*
E *Eucryphia* 'Nymansay'
F *Acer palmatum*
G *Hamamelis mollis*
H *Malus* 'John Downie'
I *Malus* 'Profusion'
J *Elaeagnus × ebbingei*
K *Elaeagnus pungens* 'Maculata'
L *Camellia* varieties.
X Wire-netting frame for leaf mould

FOR LIMY SOILS

A *Prunus lusitanica*
B *Viburnum* varieties, *Hydrangea* varieties, *Mahonia* 'Charity'
C *Buddleia davidii*
D *Stranvaesia davidiana*
E *Koelreuteria paniculata*
F *Acer palmatum*
G *Hamamelis mollis*
H *Malus* 'John Downie'
I *Malus* 'Profusion'
J *Elaeagnus × ebbingei*
K *Elaeagnus pungens* 'Maculata'
L *Viburnum farreri, Daphne pontica, Mahonia* 'Charity'
X Wire-netting frame for leaf mould

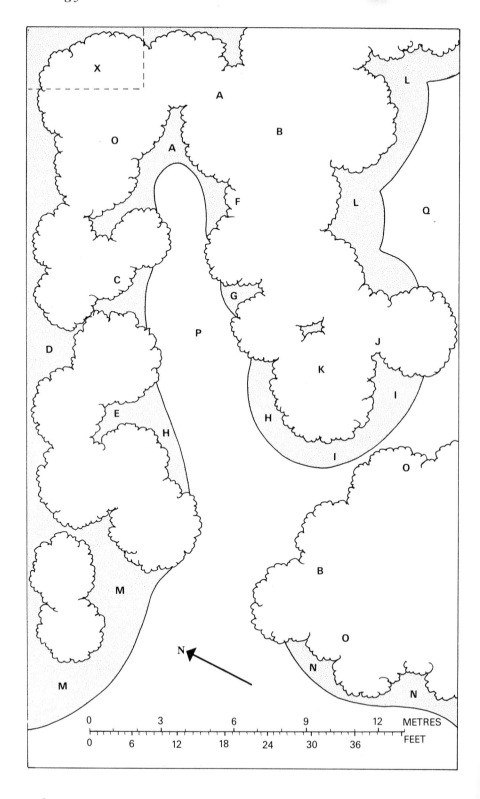

A basic planting scheme for a small plot—continued

Third Phase: FOR ACID SOILS

A Azaleas or dwarf rhododendrons
B Ground-cover herbs and bulbs
C *Ajuga reptans* 'Atropurpurea'
D *Mahonia* 'Charity'
E *Gaultheria cuneata*
F *Leucothoe fontanesiana*
G *Daphne pontica*
H *Bergenia* varieties
I *Cornus canadensis*
J *Viburnum davidii*
K *Rhododendron mucronulatum*
L Sun-loving plants
M *Hypericum calycinum*
N *Primula* varieties
O *Hosta* varieties
P Shady glade
Q Sunny glade
X Wire-netting frame for leaf mould

FOR LIMY SOILS

A *Mahonia aquifolium, M. japonica*
B Ground-cover herbs and bulbs
C *Ajuga reptans* 'Atropurpurea'
D *Mahonia* 'Charity'
E *Mahonia aquifolium*
F *Phillyrea decora*
G *Daphne pontica*
H *Bergenia* varieties
I *Polygonum affine* 'Lowndes Variety'
J *Viburnum davidii*
K *Viburnum davidii*
L Sun-loving plants
M *Hypericum calycinum*
N *Primula* varieties
O *Hosta* varieties
P Shady glade
Q Sunny glade
X Wire-netting frame for leaf mould

purple-stained flowers which start to open just as *stellata* is finishing in April, and continue through May.

Seen through the light spring tracery of *Sorbus* 'Joseph Rock', the wine-red blossom of the crab *Malus* 'Profusion' will be a focal point. Many people say this is the very best of the flowering crabs, better even than the favourite 'John Downie', with its pure white flowers, planted close behind. While 'John Downie' is losing its blossom in May, the *Amelanchier* nearby will be opening its own fragrantly white display.

Looking along this narrow, tapering glade, our eye will be drawn during April and May by the bold splash of colour from the Kurume azaleas massed at the far end, highlighted by the dark evergreen backdrop of *Prunus lusitanica*. If an alkaline soil precludes the use of azaleas, this glade is one place where the lilies can be planted to full advantage. The colour in this case will be delayed for a month or two but, I think, will be no less pleasing than the sometimes over-brilliant azaleas.

The glade is designed to 'lengthen' the garden, but it is part of the woodland; overhead and high side shade will slowly increase as the trees mature, until careful canopy thinning may become necessary in order to admit the direct rays of the sun. If conditions otherwise are right for rhododendrons and azaleas, it is the ideal site for them. Planting might proceed annually, encroaching, as it were, from the far end, until the glade is full.

Dot plants such as foxgloves should be used freely. No plants are more effective at conjuring up a woodland atmosphere and linking ground-covering shrubs and herbs with the taller bushes and trees.

Above and beyond the azaleas and to their right, the tall bushy rhododendrons, planned for a succession of bloom, are seen through the silver birch stems. There is the whole space beneath the birch crowns which I have allocated to the low carpeting plants and bulbs, but which is equally suitable for larger shade-bearing shrubs, and this could happily be declared an invasion area by rhododendrons and azaleas.

A few nurseries grow birches and other suitable trees in the form of multi-stemmed standards—clumps of two or three stems forking low down—and these are often worth a little extra, if available. They may lose in height what they have gained in bark area, but this is no bad thing in the woodland garden; one could well be used as the foremost of the birch clump in this plan.

As summer develops and the deciduous trees come into full leaf, we are able to appreciate the many variations in shape and shade, some subtle, others dramatic—a theme continued at ground level, where the many textures of the shrubs are linked by clumps of sculptured hostas and arching ferns. High summer is not the season for flower, but *Eucryphia* 'Nymansay' is a picture in white, and the buddleias bordering the sunny glade beyond the birches give an unfailing display—there are many varieties to choose from, ranging in colour from dark crimson-purple through lavender and pink shades to pure white. Buddleia is well named the butterfly bush; the common purple variety especially attracts these insects.

It is a good idea when planning a woodland garden to include a glade like this—however small—sited where it will trap the sun. There should be no hint of gloom as the trees develop and overall shade increases. Such a sunny spot is necessary also for nectar-bearing and sun-loving plants to grow, and such plants are in the majority. While woodland azaleas and rhododendrons can be allowed to overflow and fill the shady glade, this sunny glade will serve the same purpose for the many sun-seeking woodland borderers, as well as the more conventional roses and garden annuals.

Many of the ground-covering shrubs are at their best in full summer: *Hypericum calycinum* is a mass of golden yellow, often over a full four months, and the white stars of *Cornus canadensis* are starting to give way to its equally showy red berries. For a limy soil, I have suggested *Polygonum affine* 'Lowndes Variety' as a substitute for the carpeting dogwood, and this will give a fine showing of deep pink flower spikes which darken in colour as the season progresses from June to October, by which time they will have mellowed into a rich and autumnal ruby red.

The approach of autumn sees the strawberry tree, *Arbutus unedo*, coming into flower and seed in quick succession, so that both are on display at the same time. The drooping pink or white flower cups, and the odd, edible strawberry-like fruits stand out well against the evergreen darkness of the foliage. Several other trees are ripening showy fruits and berries at this time: *Sorbus* 'Joseph Rock' is a rowan with outstanding, creamy-yellow berries; *S. sargentiana* has the more traditional scarlet berries in huge bunches. The crab apple 'John Downie' is a delight to see, laden with orange and scarlet fruit. The maples have long since produced their ornamental bunches of keys, but around and beneath *Acer davidii* the deep yellow, fragrant flowers of *Mahonia* 'Charity' are set off to perfection by its glossy, holly-like leaves.

The brief glory of autumn colour from maples, rowans and the other deciduous trees soon passes, and our viewpoint takes in a winter scene. The maples are renowned for the beauty of their bark, and the species included in this plan are no exceptions.

Behind the striped bark and bare twigs of *A. davidii* in the winter is the most colourful group in the garden: the pollarded willows, with *Salix* 'Chermesina' to the left, splaying out brilliantly scarlet shoots at the crown; another of the same variety at ground level, to draw the eye down and back, this brilliant red shading into the rich orange-yellow of *S.* 'Vitellina', planted in line. These three need cutting hard back to the base of the shoots every second spring, the standard tree to the crown-junction at 1·5 m (5 ft), and the other two to a point near ground level. These bright colours are all the more pleasing when seen thus framed by 'Joseph Rock', whose pale berries still decorate the bare branches. Hungry birds seem to prefer red rowan berries to these white and yellow kinds, and they often last on the tree until spring.

For winter colour in the central block, the bright, peeling bark of *Acer griseum* and the silvery-white of the birch stems have their backing of dark green rhododendron foliage. In front of them, seen through the bare twigs of the flowering dogwood, the witch hazel flowers stand out pale yellow above the light purple of the winter-flowering *Rhododendron mucronulatum*—a subtly pleasing combination.

Near the house the camellias, in their sheltered corner, should be flowering throughout the winter months, giving an exotic touch where it is needed most, with their glorious pinks and reds—and also, perhaps, providing those floating blossom arrangements which are so admired on the dinner table. The orchid-pink 'Donation', one of the easiest of camellias to grow, has the most perfect of flowers, both in water and on the bush. Even without flowers, the glossy evergreen foliage of these camellias, with their sheltering *Elaeagnus*, will provide a solid balance to the design, without in any way impeding one's view of the woodland garden.

Index